NGAIO MARSH'S

HAMLET

THE 1943 PRODUCTION SCRIPT

For my mother, Cecily Hoskins

NGAIO MARSH'S

HAMLET

THE 1943 PRODUCTION SCRIPT

Edited with an introduction by
Polly Hoskins

CANTERBURY UNIVERSITY PRESS

UNIVERSITY OF CANTERBURY
Te Whare Wānanga o Waitaha
CHRISTCHURCH NEW ZEALAND

First published in 2019 by
CANTERBURY UNIVERSITY PRESS
University of Canterbury
Private Bag 4800, Christchurch
NEW ZEALAND
www.canterbury.ac.nz/engage/cup

Book design and layout: Smartwork Creative, www.smartworkcreative.co.nz

Front cover image: Ngaio Marsh, 1936-1937?, Christchurch, by WS Baverstock. Purchased 1999 with
New Zealand Lottery Grants Board funds. Te Papa (O.020610). Colourised by Lewis Fletcher

Printed by Your Books, Wellington

CONTENTS

ACKNOWLEDGEMENTS

We gratefully acknowledge the Alexander Turnbull Library and the Macmillan Brown Library for access to material in their possession. Thanks also to John Dacres-Mannings, copyright holder for Ngaio Marsh Estate; Dr Bruce Harding, Ngaio Marsh House; Ngā Taonga Sound & Vision; Richard Lovell-Smith Estate; and Jan Hellriegel and the team at Songbroker. For the preparation of this edition, we are indebted to Catherine Montgomery and Katrina McCallum at Canterbury University Press; Anna Rogers, our editor; and Ben Woods at Promethean Editions for computer-setting the music. For helping the project along, we wish to thank Rod Biss, Paul Bushnell, Fiona Farrell, Lewis Fletcher, Mary Lovell-Smith, Sean Lydiard, Dr Philip Norman, Aileen O'Sullivan, Tate Steele, Dr Glyn Strange and Dr Nicholas Wright. Particular thanks are due to Professor Philip Armstrong, whose supervision was the inspiration for this book.

Polly Hoskins
Robert Hoskins
Christchurch 2019

LIST OF ILLUSTRATIONS

1. The programme for the opening season. *Ngaio Marsh Collection, Alexander Turnbull Library, PA1-q-173-programme*

2. The stage design for the production. *Ngaio Marsh Collection, Alexander Turnbull Library, fMS-154-1-cyclorama*

3. Page 1 of Marsh's typescript. *Ngaio Marsh Collection, Alexander Turnbull Library, fMS-154-1-1*

4. Scene 1. Bernardo tells of seeing the ghost. *Ngaio Marsh Collection, Alexander Turnbull Library, fMS-154-1-1-verso*

5. Scene 2. Cast photo: Hamlet is set apart because of the inward journey he is making. *Ngaio Marsh Collection, Alexander Turnbull Library, PA1-q-173-3-1*

6. Scene 4. Hamlet determinedly follows his father's ghost. *Painting by Richard Lovell-Smith, courtesy of Richard Lovell-Smith Estate*

7. Scene 5. Hamlet, Horatio and Marcellus swear an oath of allegiance. *Ngaio Marsh Collection, Alexander Turnbull Library, PA1-q-173-7-2*

8. Scene 9. Hamlet lays his head on Ophelia's lap. *Ngaio Marsh Collection, Alexander Turnbull Library, fMS-154-4-36-verso*

9. Scene 9. The play within the play. *Ngaio Marsh Collection, Alexander Turnbull Library, PA1-q-173-15*

10. Scene 17. Hamlet delivers the 'Alas, poor Yorick' speech. *Ngaio Marsh Collection, Alexander Turnbull Library, PA1-q-173-21-1*

11. Scene 18. The duel that ends the play. *Ngaio Marsh Collection, Alexander Turnbull Library, PA1-q-173-2*

12. Scene 18. Soldiers march off bearing Hamlet's body. *Ngaio Marsh Collection, Alexander Turnbull Library, PA1-q-173-25*

Three-quarters of a century has passed since the ghost of the dead king first walked the battlements in Ngaio Marsh's 1943 Hamlet *at the Canterbury College Little Theatre.*[1] *Fast-paced, with a deftly cut text and presented in modern dress, the production was a hit with wartime audiences and established Marsh's reputation as a Shakespearean director. Her typescript is printed here for the first time, along with Douglas Lilburn's hitherto unpublished incidental music.*

---

1   The Little Theatre, a small ground space and gallery with seating capacity for just under 200 and a stage with a cyclorama for background lighting, was housed in the old University of Canterbury, now the Arts Centre of Christchurch. For a full account see Glyn Strange, *The Little Theatre: Golden Years of the New Zealand Stage* (Christchurch: Clerestory Press, 2000).

INTRODUCTION

The crystalline sound of three violins evokes the frosty night and a
tubular bell tolls the midnight hour as Francisco, in greatcoat and tin
helmet, turns, with his bayoneted rifle, to challenge Bernardo, who
has come to relieve him on watch. As Francisco leaves, Horatio and
Marcellus enter, warming themselves around a brazier and speaking
of the ghost Bernardo and Marcellus have seen two nights in a row.
Horatio is sceptical, but just as Bernardo indicates a star in the same
spot, the stage ghost light gleams eerily. As Bernardo speaks of 'the bell
then beating one' that heralded the ghost's appearance, it softly strikes.
All the men gasp, and rising from their huddle, point to a ghostly figure.
In hoarse whispers they recognise the ghost's likeness to the dead king,
Hamlet's father, while the spirit passes by, its figure silhouetted against
the diorama. Horatio challenges the ghost, who vanishes stage right.
Horatio murmurs of dark omens as the ghost reappears in its spooky
light. Again, Horatio challenges it to impart its message but the cock
crows while the figure moves stage left. Marcellus and Bernardo raise
their rifles to prevent the ghost's exit, but fail. Horatio, a step upstage,

declares he must tell Hamlet of the foreboding figure they have seen. *Exeunt.*

———

This was the unforgettable first scene of a significant piece of New Zealand theatre history, brought to life from Marsh's typescript, which was pasted into a large bound folder and supplemented with detailed stage directions and drawings of the stage action. These opening moments, connecting the play to the Second World War, left an indelible impression on poet Allen Curnow, who reviewed the production for the *New Zealand Listener*:

> 'Elsinore, a platform before the castle.' Francisco at his post, in tin hat and army greatcoat, armed with service rifle, bayonet fixed. As on some New Zealand coast defence post, so at Elsinore. 'Enter to him Bernardo.' – similarly accoutred. So, the very first scene gave us the literal extreme of modern dress. Against a blue-lit cyclorama the figures looked larger than life on the small stage. The familiar challenge and reply came with heightened reality – was it 'modern dress' that did it? The worst fear was past, at all events, Shakespeare's lines and the New Zealand Army having proved so little incongruous …[1]

Ngaio Marsh had been invited by the Canterbury University College Students Drama Society (CUCDS) to produce a play over an eight-week rehearsal period for performances at the end of the winter term. Two years before, she had directed Sutton Vane's *Outward Bound* for the society but even then, in an interview, the student paper *Canta* quoted her advocacy for performing Shakespeare:

> The box-office play is often a good vehicle for technique, and for this reason an amateur society should perform them as well as the less known play. Shakespeare himself is box office. He wrote for the boys in the pit,

not for the highbrow few on the stage itself. *Hamlet* in modern clothes
would be a venture for a university drama society, but it would have to
be an extremely naturalistic rendering. Breadth of treatment and an utter
lack of intellectual snobbery or self-consciousness are essential for the
acting of Shakespeare.[2]

Marsh's preference for *Hamlet* in modern dress with minimal staging
was inspired not only by the confines of the Little Theatre and a desire
to introduce the play to another generation, but also by the model
of Tyrone Guthrie's production at the Old Vic in London, with Alec
Guinness in the title role, which she had attended in 1938. She had also
been electrified by an Allan Wilkie Shakespeare Company production in
Christchurch in 1915, also in wartime.[3] *Hamlet* had direct appeal, too, for
Marsh the mystery writer, who already had an international reputation
for her crime novels.[4] After all, *Hamlet* can be seen as an Elizabethan
revenge play, the story of a murdered man whose son undertakes to
avenge his death. And producing *Hamlet* in modern dress for a student
production allowed Marsh to shine a spotlight on the most immediate
and pressing of contemporary realities when student magazines were
questioning the role of the university in wartime.[5]

Marsh brought much to the task beyond her grasp of the play's
meaning and how it might be presented in 1943. Her young cast
responded to her work habits and practical theatrical experience,
combined with a magnetic personality. One student recalled that 'she
boomed like the proverbial bittern', chain-smoking and gesturing the
parts; another observed her 'totally absorbed in her marked scripts and
scene settings'.[6] She drilled students relentlessly in rehearsal, bending
their accents to achieve a stage resonance,[7] but in a spirit of courtesy
and trust that drew the best out of them.

Nevertheless, as Elric Hooper has pointed out, although Marsh's methods seemed daringly new in Christchurch, and despite her formidable grasp of shifting modes of performance, her viewpoint was 'fundamentally Victorian'. Her 'paradigm was the theatre in which Henry Irving was king ... her basic vocabulary was that of the large proscenium stage, the large effect and the romantic gesture', so that 'the play was seen as a series of pictures and the actors placed according to the laws of painting' with 'thrilling visual climaxes'.[8] Hooper also, however, identifies some post-Victorian influences, such as the Swiss stage designer Adolphe Appia, the German director and theatre theoretician Leopold Jessner and, above all, Konstantin Stanislavsky, who directed and acted in the plays of Chekhov.[9] Stanislavsky's fundamental approach to staging inclined towards romantic melodrama: use of picturesque groupings, characterful mannerisms, pregnant pauses and atmospheric effects with music and diffused lighting to create an overpowering mood – all intended to enthral audiences. Nor did he seek to elicit organic performances from his actors. Their every move, reaction and intonation were prescribed by his promptbook and learned by rote.

Marsh not only embraced such concepts, but also Stanislavsky's dictum that a play should be dominated by a single idea. 'The first duty of the producer,' she noted, 'is to make up his mind if possible in Stanislavsky's one word what the play is about. Sometimes it jumps to the eye. *Macbeth*, he may decide, is about ambition, *Othello* about jealousy, *Hamlet* about death. But what is *Lear* about, what *The Tempest*? Within the confines of his own understanding, the producer must know.'[10] Such an approach also applied to the appearance of a production: 'In moving players about the stage, the producer will be guided by the temper of the play. He may think, perhaps, that *Hamlet* is angular in feeling, *Othello* rich, or *Private Lives* sleek ...'[11]

The casting decisions for *Hamlet* were also a key factor in the show's success. Darkly handsome, fiercely intelligent, a young man with attitude, English-born Jack Henderson, who played the title role, was, in Marsh's eyes, ideal for the part. English teacher and future lecturer in Shakespeare, Lawrence Baigent, thought him 'superb', even if others, such as John Pocock, a CUCDS member and later an internationally distinguished historian and political scientist, considered he 'was always on the verge of ranting'.[12] Henderson certainly fired up the cast, committing himself completely to Marsh's expectations. His partial lameness, the result of childhood polio, contributed to the revelation of Hamlet's vulnerability.

For Henderson, the contemporary feel of the production was all-embracing:

> The modern dress necessitated modern treatment … If done well, the broad, ye olde actore technique comes off in a costume play, but as soon as it is mounted modern the production as a whole must be treated modern. We did our best to speak trippingly on the tongue, we made the verse prose without destroying the rhythm, we made the sentiments modern and the ordinary conversations ordinary conversations instead of mouthed utterances … By not having to interest the audience with an archaic piece probably indifferently done, [we] had a fresh modern play for a modern audience.[13]

His comment suggests that Marsh's approach was modern in the sense that local context remained central. She was, perhaps, taking Shakespeare's own stylistic modernisation of dramatic speech, which is both enacted and discussed in the play itself, and reapplying it to her own production.[14]

In Marsh's view, a modern production with spare staging, rightly focused on what she called 'the interpretation of emotion by rhythmic movement and sound', meaning that the 'voice follows the pulse of [the] author's lines' and 'performance is incorporate in a pattern … [that] is essentially rhythmic'.[15] John Pocock described it this way: 'All Ngaio's Shakespearean direction was built on the *speaking of verse* by actors *moving in space*; and the cyclorama created the effect (not the illusion) of space necessary to establish the relation between *verse* and *space* … Her presentations were never static, but always very mobile, even when two-dimensional space was small and cramped. You might say there was infinite space in a nutshell.'[16]

Marsh often used the analogy of music to clarify her ideas on play production. The producer, for example, was like an orchestral conductor; the 'pace of the dialogue' should 'change as the feeling of stress grows or slackens' just like 'slow and fast passages' in music; pauses can be like 'taking false rests … when one instrument should hand on a phrase to another'; and 'inside the frame of teamwork are individual performances, just as inside the orchestral work there are the separate instrumentalists'.[17]

In terms of speaking, she required clarity, resonance and projection, and she instructed students on the aural movement of blank verse. As Jack Henderson recalled, 'The first thing was to teach me to speak blank verse … Ngaio Marsh … spent the whole afternoon with me going over about ten lines of the first soliloquy. I learnt how to breathe and how to come to a climax. I learnt how to hold myself in reserve. I learnt how to take things quietly. After that afternoon I did not look back.'[18] The typescript of the play, perhaps surprisingly, was presented not in blank verse but in prose. The idea was to prevent the player from dropping his or her voice or making 'a pause at the end of each line [and] forever coming to a stop where no stop is needed', thereby destroying the 'feel' of the rhythm and the 'sense of the word'.[19] Putting the verse into prose also encouraged characters to enter into a dialogue, creating the idea of conversation and exchange.

In her booklet *A Play Toward*, Marsh, demonstrating with the opening lines of *Hamlet*, claimed that 'if phrasing is right' then 'the door to interpretation has opened':

> 'Have you had quiet guard?'
> 'Not a mouse stirring.'
> 'Well, good-night. If you do meet Horatio and Marcellus – '
> The miracle of these lines, their stillness, comes to life when the speakers let them run quietly through without a pause until the 'Well'. The player dwells here a moment and the 'good-night' follows on a falling inflection, marking the end of the sequence. 'If you do meet' leads into a new linked passage. The character of the soldiers appears through the movement of the lines. This is always the way with Shakespeare. If you are worried about interpretation make sure you have not blundered in your phrasing.[20]

Marsh planned every detail of the production very precisely before even gathering the students for rehearsal. Her envisioning of the 'smaller and greater climaxes' of the action meant that she struck it 'rhythmically in the appointed order' to attain maximum impact.[21]

———

Hamlet ran for six nights, from Monday 2 August to Saturday 7 August 1943, to packed houses. Some students even straddled the beams in the rafters, some sat on top of the electrician's box in the auditorium and others were so close to the stage that they rested their arms on it.[22] The atmosphere pulsed with excitement and anticipation. Allen Curnow described the 'outstanding' experience to Denis Glover, who was serving in the Royal Navy: 'the best Shakespeare I've ever seen here …

The public simply clamoured for seats every night, & the students were reproved by the City Council (!) for cramming 290 into the Little Theatre instead of the permissible 200. Lilburn wrote music for three violins for entr'actes etc., which struck me as very fine.'[23]

One correspondent to the *Press* thought the play should be broadcast, saying that 'hundreds of people' were turned away because it was booked out and that the adaptation 'was presented in a form admirably suitable for radio'.[24] The paper's review commended all aspects of the production, from costumes, music, staging and skilful cutting ('with no tiresome waits and no prompting') to the actors, particularly Jack Henderson, 'who scored a triumph', but also Marie Donaldson as Gertrude, Jim Walshe as Claudius, Yvonne Westmacott as Ophelia, Paul Molineaux as Laertes, H. L. Ross as Polonius and Dundas Walker as the ghost. In all, the students' 'faith in themselves' for tackling such a rich and complex play 'was fully justified'.[25]

Curnow's review for the *Listener* was the most illuminating. He began by emphasising the significance of the students' choice to perform *Hamlet*, a play not seen in New Zealand for a generation and well overdue, and also noted that 'After the triumph scored with battledress' – in the powerful opening scene – 'modern dress had still some really difficult tests to pass'.

> The burial of Ophelia, with the women following in modern black day clothes and heavy veils, might in anticipation have seemed doomed to falsity; but again, it succeeded. Shakespeare by that time was so utterly in command of both audience and cast, that cremation might almost have been substituted without disaster. The duel, that is, the fencing match of Hamlet and Laertes, lost nothing by representation as a correctly played bout, with masks and foils and umpire, the contestants in slacks and white shirts.[26]

Not quite so laudatory was the *Canta* review by John Pocock, who seemed to feel that the attempted modernisation had not gone far enough. He thought the characters looked as if they had stepped from the pages of Anthony Hope's courtly adventure-romances *The Prisoner of Zenda* and *Rupert of Hentzau* (set in the fictional European kingdom of 'Ruritania'). Then came a complaint about too much melodrama, something modernists loathed, and tended to associate with Victorianism: '*Hamlet* cannot be made twentieth-century when that century is fundamentally anti-melodramatic … it is only a "timeless" work in the sense that it might apply to any epoch of melodrama.' Pocock labelled Henderson a 'bravura Hamlet' for his inflated declamation, insisting that 'even when his voice was quietest' there was 'no stillness'. He then took aim at the style of acting, which seemed to disobey the very instructions Hamlet gives to the players about avoiding archaic mannerisms: 'Of the subtleties and profundities so often found (or read into) Hamlet there was nothing … there were too many attitudes and sawings of the air (and that atrociously prolonged sobbing).' Pocock admitted, however, that Henderson generally 'sustained a very exhausting part and carried his point through'. He found much to admire, in particular Ophelia's 'fantasia-like' mad scene, the play within the play, and the 'silhouetted procession at the end'.[27]

Hamlet, by popular demand, enjoyed a return season from 27 November to 4 December, following end-of-year examinations. After a 1944 production of *Othello*, with Paul Molineaux in the title role and Henderson as Iago, and an Elizabethan setting with new music by Lilburn, both plays toured nationally. Marsh produced *Hamlet* again for the drama society in July 1958 with Elric Hooper in the title role but in Byronic dress.

———

The source text of this edition is Marsh's producer's text, a typescript deposited in the Alexander Turnbull Library under the call number fMS-154. It is a shortened version of Shakespeare's play, divided into 17 scenes (expanded to 18 at the last minute), meticulously marked with blocking instructions and sketches. Reinserted was Scene 14, which depicts the advance of Fortinbras's troops. It is often cut, and does not appear in the Second Quarto version, but Marsh surely realised that its absence weakened the atmosphere of imminent threat that underlies the play, from the nervous watchmen at the start to the actual invasion at the end, so pertinent to her wartime production.[28] Thanks to Marsh's habit of predefining action, the foundation typescript text of *Hamlet*, and a wealth of publicity photographs, it is possible to reconstruct what happened on stage with some degree of certainty.[29]

In her booklet *Play Production*, Marsh speaks of the producer's script as a map or guidebook or orchestral score. 'It is the thing itself, it is your author, almost in person.'[30] In *A Play Toward*, she advises creating a script that 'should leave plenty of room for notes. A typed script on one side of foolscap pages, bound horizontally, with wide margins none too big', which is an exact description of fMS-154. She then elaborates on the role of the script in a passage that memorably conveys the contribution of her painterly imagination:

> You will first of all absorb the form and feel of the play – what, fundamentally, it is about. As you do this a host of ideas about the characters, the setting, the colour and the movement of the play, will begin to form themselves about your root-impression. You will begin to see and hear the play. Presently you will be ready to find its precise shape. It may curve upwards to a central major climax and down to a

final resolution. Its greatest moments may, on the contrary, be delayed until the last scene. Having found the broad shape, you will look for the forms within this shape; the minor climaxes and, within the passages leading to these, the smaller and smallest stresses. You will mark all such passages with any notes that seem essential, keeping their relation to each other balanced and controlled.[31]

Marsh studied at the Canterbury College School of Art and by the 1930s she was exhibiting with The Group, an avant-garde collective of Christchurch artists who absorbed theories of modernism, learning how to construct space in a landscape painting and schematising the forms. It is no surprise, then, that her blocking diagrams create a general effect of rhythmic movement as figures shift towards and away from one other; occasionally they are seen from behind, emphasising the spontaneous nature of the scene; at other times Hamlet is placed on the periphery of the court circle, symbolising his feelings of alienation.

In Scene 1 of Marsh's typescript, Bernardo and Marcellus, on night watch at the castle, wish to convince Hamlet's friend Horatio that they have seen the ghost of the dead king, Hamlet's father. When the ghost appears to Horatio, he decides to tell Hamlet. Marsh provides, along with written instructions, 13 sketches to depict stage movement that achieve an almost cinematic impression. To begin the sequence, Francisco stands alone upstage in a Second World War soldier's uniform, with his back to the audience. He turns to face Bernardo, challenging him with his bayoneted rifle.[32] They relax when they recognise each other and idly stand close together before Francisco shoulders his weapon and descends the steps to go off duty (see illustration 3). Horatio and Marcellus enter stage right. Marcellus and Bernardo confer while Horatio warms his hands at a brazier central front stage. At 'sit we down', they all gather around the fire. Bernardo, in the middle, relates the sighting of the ghost. (A second, enlarged sketch details this moment. See illustration 4.) Blocking text tells us that Marcellus 'sees a ghost light on Horatio, hears the bell and turns right'; all three stand in alarm pointing to the ghost, stage right, and Horatio moves forward to speak to it.

When the ghost disappears, the three men talk, Horatio and Bernardo standing upstage with Marcellus directly below them on the steps. Marcellus and Bernardo look toward Horatio as he delivers his 'bodes some strange eruption' speech. The ghost reappears and Horatio speaks but is interrupted by the cock crowing. The soldiers raise their rifles to stop the ghost's departure, and written instructions indicate movement up and down the steps when Marcellus asks, 'Shall I strike at it?' They huddle again after the ghost's exit, then separate as Horatio greets the dawn: he stands up centre at the point where he determines to confront the ghost. The movement throughout emphasises knotted groupings that highlight both the presence of potential menace and the need to guard against it.

The image of Francisco at his post with his back to the audience creates an immediate sense of ambiguity. Gathering round the brazier conveys the idea of protective warmth and light against the surrounding darkness. The eerie ghost light and the striking bell electrify the three men, who leap to their feet and point at the 'dreaded sight' that 'harrows' them with 'fear and wonder'. Horatio moves to address the ghost a second time, but the cock crows, leaving the trio to cluster again.

Scene 2 offers the direct contrast of a brightly lit court, where Claudius begins proceedings with a forked-tongued speech. A sketch depicts a stately, formal image of him and Queen Gertrude seated at a table upstage, framed by courtiers. Hamlet, however, is seated in a chair front stage, facing Claudius but, like Francisco earlier, with his back to the audience. He is the one discordant figure, distanced and opposed to the royal group. At Claudius's first question, 'How is it that the clouds still hang on you?', Hamlet stands and raises his hands as he replies, 'I am too much i' the sun.' When Hamlet speaks to his mother about his 'suits of solemn black' – his costume is in stark contrast to the colourful show of the court – he turns to the audience for the first time to deliver the loaded phrase, 'but I have that within which passeth show', a clear rebuttal of Claudius's double-talk. A cast photograph of this moment captures Hamlet's separateness from a bewildered court; his manner meditative, as befits a scholar whose watchword is 'truth' (see illustration 5). From the outset, Hamlet is characterised as one of those 'alienated consciousnesses' in which modernism was so interested.

Other sketches in the prompt script show that Hamlet 'flinches' when Claudius places a hand on his shoulder; that he stands sulkily, head bowed, with his back to the king and queen; and that Gertrude embraces Hamlet (showing her fondness for her son) as she begs him to stay, while Claudius draws apart from them (underlining his antagonism). For his first soliloquy, Hamlet moves to the table, sits at it, picks up a document, rises again and moves front stage, expressing his shifting moods of bewilderment and frustration. If Claudius's hand on Hamlet's shoulder makes him shudder, Horatio's, at 'My lord, I think I saw him yesternight', conveys the sharing of a confidence, as does the naturalistic dialogue that follows, and when Hamlet dismisses his companions he 'places his hands on their shoulders' in comradeship and trust.

In Scene 3, Polonius bids farewell to his son Laertes, and both men warn Ophelia against Hamlet's courtship. At the beginning, Laertes, ready to leave, places his dispatch case on a stool before turning to speak to his sister. With her opening line, Ophelia helps him to put on his coat.

Later, following the end of his 'blessing' speech, Polonius 'claps Laertes on the arms' before he departs. Polonius then sits in a chair and selects a cigar and picks up matches, as he cautions his daughter. He lights up at 'Give me up the truth', and, as shown in a sketch, Ophelia sits on the stool beside her father. In his speech ending the scene, Polonius chucks his daughter under the chin at 'the soul lends the tongue vows' and, as he finishes, stands and holds out his hand to her; she rises in response and 'goes to him'. The lighting is unchanged from the previous scene but the blocking, in sharp contrast to that between Hamlet, his mother and Claudius, focuses on a close family unit with gestures of affectionate reassurance counterpointing loving words of advice. A young man going away from home clearly relates to the experience of wartime families.

At the beginning of the second ghost scene, tension mounts as Hamlet waits impatiently: he looks at his watch, walks towards the brazier, then paces up and down while the court revelry is heard in the background. Hamlet moves centre front stage when the ghost bell strikes but backs away at the spirit's entrance. When the ghost beckons, Hamlet advances stage right but is restrained by the others; he struggles free by slipping out of his cloak, which is 'left in Horatio's hands'. The movement confirms that his determination to encounter the ghost cannot be resisted, which in turn tells us that Hamlet will not veer from the truth. Richard Lovell-Smith's painting of this moment shows a soldierly Hamlet clasping his sword in its scabbard as an added gesture of determination (see illustration 6).

Falling on the steps before the ghost, Hamlet hears the revelation of his father's murder and, at the end of the scene, he, Horatio and Marcellus kneel as they swear an oath of allegiance (see illustration 7), placing their hands on one another's. In the soliloquy ending Scene 7, 'O, what a rogue and peasant slave am I', Hamlet fingers the pieces of a chess set on the table. When he calls Claudius a 'bloody, bawdy villain!', he picks up the king chessman, laughs ironically and puts it down. The link to chess is there, too, in the final words: 'the play's the thing wherein I'll catch the conscience of the King.' Hamlet is embroiled in a complex psychological game and he has been thinking ahead to some purpose about how to foil Claudius.

There are no blocking indications for Hamlet's 'To be, or not to be' soliloquy in the 'nunnery' scene, which suggests that he stands very still to speak words of such indeterminable depth. By contrast, when Hamlet and Ophelia converse obliquely, the movement between them is cast in subtle shifts that suggest a tension that both magnetises and repels. When Hamlet finally makes his exit, for example, 'Ophelia tries to follow him, but collapses on steps': this disquieting gesture is a striking depiction of her distress and his bitterness, which breaks their bond while magnifying it.

The central climax of *Hamlet* is the play within the play in Scene 9. When Claudius enters, he finds Hamlet casually smoking a cigarette, which he stubs out when he cynically speaks to Ophelia of the brevity of woman's love, a gesture that again identifies Hamlet as an outsider. Here Lilburn's plaintive music begins and continues until the moment of murder, when 'silence' is cued. At the start of this sequence Hamlet is sketched lying with his head on Ophelia's lap (see illustration 8) but the scene ends in a sort of noisy coda (see illustration 9), with Claudius's abrupt departure and all calling for 'lights'. The effect is somewhat like the strong colours and modern anxieties represented in an expressionist painting. For the following scene, a sketch shows Claudius kneeling at a prayer desk, Hamlet behind him with a drawn sword, but a cast photograph reveals the king, dressed in a confessional gown, leaning over a chair.

The scene where Hamlet quarrels with his mother includes many blocking indications aimed at underlining its emotional intensity. Sometimes the stage action is shocking, for example when Hamlet brutally pushes his mother towards the looking glass, 'forcing her down' into a chair at the words 'rash, intruding fool' and apparently holding a candle close to her face as she weeps. Later, when Ophelia distributes flowers in her 'mad' scene, there is a subtle echo of Gertrude's awakening knowledge of Claudius's menace: Ophelia passes from the ladies at court to the queen to Horatio but when she nears the king, she screams and quickly returns centre stage.

The graveyard scene is alive with illustrative sketches and action cues. There is also a photograph of the moment that Hamlet examines Yorick's skull. Standing at the grave edge, he gazes intently at what remains of the former jester while Horatio, arms folded, looks on and the gravediggers rest, a beer bottle at the ready. A stone angel and sunken cross provide funereal imagery (see illustration 10). The manuscript sketches tell us that the scene begins with the sight of two shovels casting up earth then the gravediggers are depicted leaning on their tools to chat; text cues indicate when they spit on their hands to prevent blisters and suck their teeth in noisy anticipation of liquid refreshment. Later sketches depict Hamlet smoking while in casual conversation with the sexton and the latter handing over Yorick's skull. The entry of the funeral party is followed by the bearers lowering Ophelia's coffin into the grave. The gravediggers advance to fill the grave but Laertes interrupts them. Hamlet, in a blaze of passion, leaves his cloak with Horatio in order to attack Laertes: in a highly dramatic moment, courtiers seize Laertes and Horatio, and the priest draw Hamlet away.

Blocking for the final scene begins with a lengthy cue: 'Hamlet gives Horatio's arm a shake; down steps; they hear voices [those attending the fencing match]; Hamlet turns back on the audience [an echo of Francisco's stance at the very beginning and of the first view of Hamlet], braces himself and faces upstage; Court enter.' When Claudius greets Hamlet, he clicks his heels – for the 1940s audience an association with Hitler's Nazis doing the same when they saluted – and bows. The preparation for the duel has instructions for testing foils and buttoning up tunics, and when Osric steps up to referee, the duellists salute each other before beginning 'play on fore stage' (see illustration 11). A servant brings in the poisoned cup intended for Claudius, from which Gertrude drinks in toast to her son. After the first bout, she wipes the sweat from Hamlet's face: he bows 'gallantly' to her and kneels as she 'reaches out her hand with handkerchief'. The swordplay continues and both players are wounded. As Horatio tends to Hamlet and Osric to Laertes, Gertrude stands, then 'falls back'; a lady in waiting 'stoops over the Queen'; Laertes is assisted to the steps stage left and Hamlet 'breaks from Horatio and up steps to face Queen'. Hamlet, mortally wounded, musters up the strength to stab Claudius before dropping his sword. The lady in waiting screams as Hamlet 'staggers back from the King'.

In a cast photograph, Horatio, centre stage, gazes at the dying Hamlet and Osric cradles Laertes' body. Hamlet's last gesture has been to prevent Horatio from committing suicide by drinking the poisoned cup which he seizes – 'here's yet some liquor left' – urging his friend to live so that he may tell the truth about what has occurred. As Hibbard observes, looking back over the play 'from the vantage point of the final scene', one begins to see 'a skeleton of allegory … a struggle between Falsehood and Deception, embodied in the King, and Truth, embodied in the Prince'.[33] Marsh seems acutely aware of such a skeleton, though for her audience it can perhaps be interpreted as a struggle for national identity in wartime. The point is made clear in a cast photograph (see illustration 12), reproduced as a lino-cut by Roy Dickison for *Review* 1943, depicting the dead Hamlet carried on a stretcher by four helmeted soldiers. The caption reads 'Let four captains bear Hamlet, like a soldier, to the stage'. This could be a scene from El Alamein or Cassino. Those words, originally spoken by Fortinbras the invader, are instead given to Horatio. (Fortinbras was removed from the production, possibly considered too threatening, in 1943, to appear in as positive a light as he does in the full play.) Nevertheless, by being carried out with 'soldiers' music, and the rites of war', Hamlet is granted heroic status. He has resisted Claudius and purged the evil he has spread through the land.

Marsh's blocking echoes and accentuates the dramatic high points of the play: the densely atmospheric opening scene, the repressed passion exploding in violent outbursts of the quarrel scene, Hamlet shedding his coat to follow the ghost, Claudius's hasty departure from the play, Ophelia collapsing on the steps, a grieving Hamlet attacking Laertes in the grave, the duel and stabbing in the final scene. Marsh expresses often fleeting or half-recognised passions through gestures – a slight shudder, rising in alarm, a meaningful glance, a head held in hands, a scream, a clicking of heels, a whisper, holding up a candle, fingering a chessboard, stubbing out a cigarette – building up a dissonant undercurrent that is eventually released in the carnage of the final scene. *Hamlet*, in Marsh's view, is clearly a play that leaves its 'chief moment of climax' to the end.[34]

———

Marsh reduced the play to 18 scenes, partly so that the audience could catch the last tram that left Cathedral Square at 10.30 p.m. but chiefly because she wanted to present an economical student-friendly version. A full-length *Hamlet* lasts more than twice the length of Marsh's version of two hours with a single eight-minute interval. She had the confidence to cut because she had 'a clear, burning picture' of how she wanted it to be played [35] – by those particular students, in that particular theatre, and for an audience she wanted to excite. The students also felt they owned the play itself, since Marsh had created a special version just for them.[36]

According to Elric Hooper, Marsh preferred the Folio edition of *Hamlet* as the basis for her 1943 production but an examination of fMS-154 reveals it is a compound text from the Second Quarto and the Folio.[37] As he notes,

> The cutting of texts was commonplace and there was no feeling that by doing so one might distort the author's intention or transform the thematic content of the play by such foreshortening. The Shakespeare plays that Henry Irving and Ngaio's parents performed were cut by about a third, Ngaio actually owned a book, published in the early years of this [the twentieth] century, that listed traditional cuts to Shakespeare's text. And I still own a complete edition of Shakespeare, edited by Henry Irving, that has brackets round those passages that may be omitted for the purpose of playing.[38]

A comparison with Irving's nineteenth-century edition of *Hamlet* confirms that this was Marsh's copy-text for fMS-154[39] but she does not slavishly follow his recommendations. Irving, for example, bracketed anything salacious – such as the ghost's references, in Act I Scene 5, to the 'shameful lust' that will 'sate itself in a celestial bed' – whereas Marsh, producing her version post-Freud, made different decisions, using her own judgement. As she observes in *Play Production*, cutting 'is a ticklish job' requiring a 'good ear'. Her general rule was to delete superfluous scenes (those that one feels are a result of others who 'have monkeyed about with the text') and then focus on 'secondary parts' that 'can be shortened or even telescoped without interfering with the march of events'.[40] For her *Hamlet*, Marsh conflated Act IV, Scenes 2 and 3, cut then reinstated Act IV, Scene 4, and deleted Act IV, Scene 6 (Hamlet's letter to Horatio giving an account of his return to Denmark). As well as Fortinbras, she dispensed with the roles of Voltemand and Cornelius, much of Reynaldo, and chunks of Rosencrantz and Guildenstern.

A significant cut is the removal of Horatio's account, in the opening scene, of old Hamlet's invasions in border wars with Norway. This suppresses the realisation, a strong one in the full text, that Fortinbras wishes to take revenge for initial Danish aggression. In 1943 it was vital for Marsh to make his military threat seem more gratuitous, so that audiences could identify with the threatened Danes. Without the characters of Fortinbras and the Norwegian ambassador Voltemand, she was left with a more generalised sense of possible invasion. Apparently at the last minute, she included the short fourteenth scene that depicts advancing troops, identified as Fortinbras's, but conveying more the idea of a widespread threat. It may seem odd that Marsh snipped out details of territorial invasions in a wartime production, but it should be remembered that Norway and Denmark were then under German occupation. She lets military costuming and the shadowy approach of armies do the job of establishing a sense of a society at war.

More generally, other cuts serve to strengthen the overall emotional intensity. Much of Hamlet's banter, for example, is excised, which diminishes the profile of Rosencrantz and Guildenstern and elevates Polonius to someone more genuinely worthy of respect than in the full play. Other cuts are ones commonly made, such as the long account of Priam's murder, some of the ghost's lamentations, the players' 'dumb show' and the 'Rugged Pyrrhus' speech. Interestingly, most of the king's 'prayer' is jettisoned, which arguably erodes the sustained dramatic irony of Claudius finding he cannot pay the price demanded by true repentance and Hamlet sparing his enemy because he appears to be regretting his sins. Marsh always has her eye on driving the action to a climax. In the play within the play, for example, she cuts everything after Claudius cries out for 'lights', in order to leave the audience hanging, and the final scene leaves out large portions of the Hamlet–Horatio and Hamlet–Osric dialogue, and the King's 'stoups of wine' speech, to keep things moving towards the fatal duel.

Marsh's wartime *Hamlet* can perhaps be seen as part of a national attempt to keep alive the hope of community or at least the fundamental values on which community depends. Her cutting is intended to push things forward to the play within the play at the mid-point and then to the duel scene at the end, to free the dialogue from some of its intricate elaborations and to hold the interest of the audience and to focus on a connection with the present historical moment. *Hamlet*'s final bloodbath must have had added resonance for a New Zealand wartime audience and been almost unbearably moving.

NOTES

1   *New Zealand Listener*, 20 August 1943, pp. 6–7.

2   'Dramatic Potentialities of CUC [interview with Ngaio Marsh]', *Canta* (Vol. 12, No. 2), 18 September 1941, p. 7.

3   For an account of this seminal experience – 'The opening night of *Hamlet* was the most enchanted I was ever to spend in the theatre' – see Ngaio Marsh, *Black Beech and Honeydew: An Autobiography* (Auckland: Collins,1966; revised 1981), pp. 123–25. Marsh toured with the company in 1920, playing minor roles.

4   Featuring super-sleuth Chief Inspector Roderick Alleyn. For the influence of Shakespeare in Marsh's novels, see Mary S. Weinkauf, *Murder Most Poetic: The Mystery Novels of Ngaio Marsh* (San Bernadino: Brownstone Books, 2007), pp. 71–102.

5   As, for example, a spirited article in *Canta* (Vol. 13, No. 1), 17 March, 1942, entitled 'Backwards and Forwards – You Must Decide Now', asking if the university should close during wartime; if 'winning the war' was all that mattered; if the university was even more necessary, vital, than in peacetime.

6   From an account by Jim Walshe, who played Claudius, in Glyn Strange, *The Little Theatre*, p. 78; R. S. Gormack, *Diary for 1942–43* (Christchurch: Nag's Head Press, 1991), p. 6.

7   Marsh was retrospectively criticised for advocating what she called 'the voice beautiful' over the flat New Zealand accent but in 1940s Christchurch English-style diction may have been expected.

8   Marsh was a trained painter and a member of The Group, a collective of contemporary Christchurch artists.

9   Elric Hooper, 'Ngaio Marsh: A Life in Theatre', in Carole Acheson and Carol Lidgard (eds), *Return to Black Beech: Papers from a Centenary Symposium on Ngaio Marsh 1895–1995* (Christchurch: The Centre for Continuing Education, University of Canterbury), pp. 7–20. Hooper's essay presents Marsh as a unique force in New Zealand theatre while also observing her reluctance to change with the times. Henry Irving's edition of *Hamlet* (1890) became a proto-text for Marsh's typescript.

10 Ngaio Marsh, *Three Talks on Theatre: The Audience* (1952, Sound Archives/ Ngā Taonga Korero 32953), quoted in

Paul Bushnell, 'The Most Ephemeral of Arts', in *Centenary Symposium*, p. 85.

11 Ngaio Marsh, *A Play Toward* (Christchurch: Caxton Press, 1946), p. 14.

12 Quoted in Paul Bushnell, 'A Theatrical Avocation' in B. J. Rahn (ed.), *Ngaio Marsh: The Woman and her Work* (New Jersey & London: Scarecrow Press, 1995), p. 55. Baigent, a friend of both Marsh and Lilburn, used to describe *Hamlet* as 'an intense and lonely tragedy'; John Pocock, 'Hamlet of Hentzau', *Canta* (Vol. 14, No. 10), 19 August 1943, p. 4.

13 *Review*, 1944. Quoted in Strange, *The Little Theatre*, p. 79.

14 G. R. Hibbard, in the Oxford introduction to the play (p. 30), makes the point that the style of speech Shakespeare gives to Hamlet is flexible and 'modern'; 'the newness of what the playwright was now doing … is to be found in the tragedy's language … Furthermore, many of the [words] were new not only in the context of Shakespeare's work but also in the context of the English language as a whole.'

15 Ngaio Marsh, *A Play Toward*, pp. 10–11.

16 Letter to Paul Bushnell, 17 February 1984, quoted in Strange, *The Little Theatre*, p. 81.

17 Ngaio Marsh, *Play Production* (Wellington: School Publications Branch, Education Department, 1948; revised 1960), pp. 23, 25.

18 *Review*, 1944. Quoted in Strange, *The Little Theatre*, p. 81.

19 Ngaio Marsh, *Play Production*, p. 32.

20 Marsh, *A Play Toward*, p. 13.

21 Ibid.

22 Ngaio Marsh, *Black Beech and Honeydew*, p. 243.

23 Allen Curnow to Denis Glover, 14 August 1943. Quoted in Peter Simpson, *Bloomsbury South: The Arts in Christchurch 1933–1953* (Auckland: Auckland University Press, 2016), p. 142. As always in New Zealand at this time, the cultural judgements operated with an implied 'parent' culture in mind.

24 *Press*, 10 August 1943, p. 6.

25 *Press*, 4 August 1943, p. 5.

26 *New Zealand Listener*, 20 August 1943, pp. 6–7.

27 'Hamlet of Hentzau', *Canta* (Vol. 14, No. 10), 19 August 1943, p. 4.

28 Unfortunately there are no blocking images or publicity photos for this short scene (nor particular comment in reviews), so we do not know how Fortinbras's troops were uniformed.

29 Photograph albums related to the production, formerly in possession of Ngaio Marsh and Douglas Lilburn, are deposited in the Alexander Turnbull Library under the call numbers PA1-q-173, PA1-q-142, PA1-q-143.

30 Ngaio Marsh, *Play Production*, p. 8.

31 Ngaio Marsh, *A Play Toward*, pp. 20–21.

32 Most likely a Lee-Enfield, the standard rifle used by the New Zealand infantry (Tate Steele in conversation with Polly Hoskins, 2018).

33 Hibbard, *Hamlet*, p. 63.

34 Ngaio Marsh, *Play Production*, p. 9.

35 Ibid., p. 7.

36 According to Paul Molineaux, who played Laertes, quoted in Strange, *The Little Theatre*, p. 88.

37 Elric Hooper, 'The Inaugural Ngaio Marsh Lecture', 22 April 2012, p. 6.

38 Elric Hooper, 'Ngaio Marsh: A Life in Theatre', p. 16.

39 Marsh was undoubtedly aware of more recent editions as well, including Dover Wilson's of 1934 and G. B. Harrison's of 1937.

40 Ngaio Marsh, *Play Production*, p. 7.

SUGGESTED READING

Acheson, Carole and Carolyn Lidgard (eds), *The Return to Black Beech: Papers from a Centenary Symposium on Ngaio Marsh 1895–1995*. Christchurch: The Centre of Continuing Education, University of Canterbury, 1996.

Drayton, Joanne. *Ngaio Marsh: Her Life in Crime*. Auckland: HarperCollins, 2008.

Gormack, R. S. *Diary for 1942–43*. Christchurch: Nag's Head Press, 1991.

Harris, Valerie and Philip Norman (eds), *Douglas Lilburn: A Festschrift for Douglas Lilburn on his retirement from the Victoria University of Wellington, January 31, 1980*, 2nd edition. Wellington: Composers Association of New Zealand, 1980.

Hibbard, G. R. (ed.), 'General Introduction' to William Shakespeare, *Hamlet*, The Oxford Shakespeare. Oxford and New York: Oxford University Press, 1987, 1994.

Irving, Henry and Frank Marshall (eds), The Henry Irving Shakespeare. *The Works of William Shakespeare*, Volume 8 [*Hamlet*], London, Edinburgh and Glasgow: 1890.

Marsh, Ngaio. *Black Beech and Honeydew: An Autobiography*. Auckland: Collins, 1966; revised 1981.

Marsh, Ngaio. *Play Production.* Wellington: School Publications Branch, Education Department, 1948; revised 1960.

Marsh, Ngaio. *A Play Toward*. Christchurch: Caxton Press, 1946.

Ngaio Marsh Organisation. 'The Inaugural Ngaio Marsh Lecture: Elric J. Hooper, MBE, 22 April, 2012.' Accessed September 3, 2018. http://www.ngaio-marsh.org.nz/THE%20NGAIO%20MARSH%20LECTURE%202013.pdf

Norman, Philip. *Douglas Lilburn: His Life and Music*. Christchurch: Canterbury University Press, 2006.

Rahn, B. J. (ed.), *Ngaio Marsh: The Woman and her Work.* New Jersey & London: Scarecrow Press, 1995.

Simpson, Peter. *Bloomsbury South: The Arts in Christchurch 1933–1953*. Auckland: Auckland University Press, 2016.

Strange, Glyn. *The Little Theatre: Golden Years of the New Zealand Stage*. Christchurch: Clerestory Press, 2000.

Weinkauf, Mary S. *Murder Most Poetic: The Mystery Novels of Ngaio Marsh*. San Bernadino: Brownstone Books, 2007.

DRAMATIS PERSONAE

HAMLET, Prince of Denmark

GHOST, of Hamlet's father, the late King Hamlet of Denmark

KING Claudius, of Denmark, brother of the late King

QUEEN Gertrude, Hamlet's mother and his father's widow, now married
to King Claudius

POLONIUS, King Claudius's councillor

LAERTES, Polonius's son

OPHELIA, Polonius's daughter

REYNALDO, Polonius's servant

HORATIO, Hamlet's friend and fellow student

ROSENCRANTZ }
GUILDENSTERN } fellow students

OSRIC, a courtier

BERNARDO }
FRANCISCO } soldiers
MARCELLUS }

PLAYERS, including Prologue, Player King, Player Queen, Player Lucianus

FIRST CLOWN, a gravedigger

SECOND CLOWN, his crony

PRIEST

Lords, Ladies, Courtiers, Officers, Soldiers, Messengers, Attendants

HAMLET

The action of the play takes place in and around Kronborg Castle at Elsinore in Denmark.

ACT I

SCENE 1 'FIRST BATTLEMENT'

The battlements of the castle. Francisco at his post, enter Bernardo.

BERNARDO: Who's there?

FRANCISCO: Nay, answer me: stand and unfold yourself.

BERNARDO: Long live the King!

FRANCISCO: Bernardo?

BERNARDO: He.

FRANCISCO: You come most carefully upon your hour.

BERNARDO: 'Tis now struck twelve: get thee to bed, Francisco.

FRANCISCO: For this relief much thanks: 'tis bitter cold, and I am sick
    at heart.

BERNARDO: Have you had quiet guard?

FRANCISCO: Not a mouse stirring.

BERNARDO: Well, good night. If you do meet Horatio and Marcellus, the rivals of my watch, bid them make haste.

FRANCISCO: I think I hear them. – Stand! Who's there?

Enter Horatio and Marcellus.

HORATIO: Friends to this ground.

MARCELLUS: And liegemen to the Dane.

FRANCISCO: Give you good night.

MARCELLUS: O, farewell honest soldier: who hath relieved you?

FRANCISCO: Bernardo hath my place. Give you good night.

Exit Francisco.

MARCELLUS: Holla! Bernardo!

BERNARDO: Say, what, is Horatio there?

HORATIO: A piece of him.

BERNARDO: Welcome, Horatio: welcome, good Marcellus.

MARCELLUS: What, has this thing appeared again tonight?

BERNARDO: I have seen nothing.

MARCELLUS: Horatio says 'tis but our fantasy, and will not let belief take hold of him touching this dreaded sight, twice seen of us: therefore I have entreated him along with us to watch the minutes of this night; that, if again this apparition come, he may approve our eyes, and speak to it.

HORATIO: Tush, tush, 'twill not appear.

BERNARDO: Sit down awhile; and let us once again assail your ears, that are so fortified against our story, what we two nights have seen.

HORATIO: Well, sit we down, and let us hear Bernardo speak of this.

BERNARDO: Last night of all, when yond same star, that's westward from the pole had made his course to illume that part of heaven where now it burns, Marcellus and myself, the bell then beating one –

MARCELLUS: Peace! Break thee off: – look, where it comes again!

Enter Ghost.

BERNARDO: In the same figure, like the King that's dead.

MARCELLUS: Thou art a scholar; speak to it, Horatio.

BERNARDO: Looks it not like the King? Mark it, Horatio.

HORATIO: Most like: it harrows me with fear and wonder.

BERNARDO: It would be spoke to.

MARCELLUS: Question it, Horatio.

HORATIO: What art thou, that usurp'st this time of night, together
    with that fair and warlike form in which the majesty of buried
    Denmark did sometimes march? By heaven, I charge thee, speak!

MARCELLUS: It is offended.

BERNARDO: See, it stalks away.

HORATIO: Stay! Speak, speak! I charge thee, speak!

Exit Ghost.

MARCELLUS: 'Tis gone, and will not answer.

BERNARDO: How now Horatio? You tremble and look pale: is not this
    something more than fantasy? What think you on't?

HORATIO: Before my God, I might this not believe, without the sensible
    and true avouch of mine own eyes.

MARCELLUS: Is it not like the King?

HORATIO: As thou art to thyself: 'tis strange!

MARCELLUS: Thus, twice before, and jump[1] at this dead hour, with
    martial stalk hath he gone by our watch.

HORATIO: In what particular thought to work I know not; but, in the
    gross and scope of my opinion, this bodes some strange eruption
    to our state. A mote it is to trouble the mind's eye. In the most
    high and palmy state of Rome, a little ere the mightiest Julius

---

1   'Just' in some editions.

fell, the graves stood tenantless and the sheeted dead did squeak and gibber in the Roman streets; and even the like precurse of fierce events, as harbingers preceding still the fates, and prologue to the omen coming on, have heaven and earth together demonstrated unto our climatures and countrymen.

Re-enter Ghost.

But soft, behold! Lo, where it comes again! I'll cross it, though it blast me. – Stay, illusion! If thou hast any sound or use of voice, speak to me: if there be any good to be done, that may to thee do ease, and grace to me, speak to me: if thou art privy to thy country's fate, which, happily foreknowing may avoid, O, speak!

The cock crows.

Stay and speak! – Stop it, Marcellus.

MARCELLUS: Shall I strike at it?

HORATIO: Do, if it will not stand.

BERNARDO: 'Tis here!

HORATIO: 'Tis here!

Exit Ghost.

MARCELLUS: 'Tis gone! We do it wrong, being so majestical, to offer it the show of violence.

BERNARDO: It was about to speak when the cock crew.

HORATIO: And then it started, like a guilty thing upon a fearful summons. I have heard the cock, that is the trumpet to the morn, doth with his lofty and shrill-sounding throat awake the god of day; and at his warning, whether in sea or fire, in earth or air, the extravagant and erring spirit hies to his confine; and of the truth herein this present object made probation.

MARCELLUS: It faded on the crowing of the cock. Some say, that ever 'gainst that season comes wherein our Saviour's birth is celebrated, this bird of dawning singeth all night long: and then, they say, no spirit can walk abroad; the nights are wholesome; then no planets strike; no fairy takes, nor witch hath power to charm; so hallowed and so gracious is the time.

HORATIO: So have I heard, and do in part believe it. But, look, the morn, in russet mantle clad, walks o'er the dew of yon high eastern hill. Break we our watch up; and, by my advice, let us impart what we have seen tonight unto young Hamlet; for, upon my life, this spirit, dumb to us, will speak to him.

Exeunt.

SCENE 2 'FIRST COUNCIL'

The Council Chamber in the castle. Enter the King, Queen, Polonius, Laertes, Lords and Attendants.

KING: Though yet of Hamlet our dear brother's death the memory be green; and that it us befitted to bear our hearts in grief, and our whole kingdom to be contracted in one brow of woe; yet so far hath discretion fought with nature, that we with wisest sorrow think on him, together with remembrance of ourselves. Therefore our sometime sister, now our queen, the imperial jointress to this warlike state, have we, as 'twere with a defeated joy, – taken to wife: nor have we herein barred your better wisdom, which have freely gone with this affair along. For all, our thanks. And now, Laertes, what's the news with you? You told us of some suit; what is't Laertes?

LAERTES: My dread lord, your leave and favour to return to France; from whence though willingly I came to Denmark to show my duty in your coronation; yet now, I must confess, that duty done,

my thoughts and wishes bend again toward France, and bow
them to your gracious leave and pardon.

KING: Have you your father's leave? What says Polonius?

POLONIUS: He hath, my lord, wrung from me my slow leave. I do
beseech you, give him leave to go.

KING: Take thy fair hour, Laertes, time be thine, and thy best graces
spend it at thy will! But now, my cousin Hamlet and my son –

HAMLET: (*Aside*) A little more than kin, and less than kind.

KING: How is it that the clouds still hang on you?

HAMLET: Not so, my lord, I am too much i' the sun.

QUEEN: Good Hamlet, cast thy nighted colour off, and let thine eye look
like a friend on Denmark. Do not, for ever, with thy vailed lids
seek for thy noble father in the dust; thou know'st 'tis common –
all that lives must die, passing through nature to eternity.

HAMLET: Ay, madam, it is common.

QUEEN: If it be, why seems it so particular with thee?

HAMLET: Seems, madam? Nay, it is; I know not 'seems'. 'Tis not alone
my inky cloak, good mother, nor customary suits of solemn
black, together with all forms, moods, shows of grief, that can
denote me truly. These, indeed, seem, for they are actions that
a man might play; but I have that within which passeth show;
these but the trappings and the suits of woe.

KING: 'Tis sweet and commendable in your nature, Hamlet, to give
these mourning duties to your father; but, you must know, your
father lost a father; that father lost, lost his; and the survivor
bound in filial obligation for some term to do obsequious
sorrow: but to persevere in obstinate condolement is a course of
impious stubbornness; 'tis unmanly grief. We pray you, throw to
earth this unprevailing woe; and think of us as of a father: for let

the world take note, you are the most immediate to our throne, our chiefest courtier, cousin, and our son.

QUEEN: Let not thy mother lose her prayers, Hamlet: I pray thee, stay with us; go not to Wittenberg.

HAMLET: I shall in all my best obey you, madam.

KING: Why, 'tis a loving and a fair reply: be as ourself in Denmark.
– Madam, come; this gentle and unforced accord of Hamlet sits smiling to my heart: in grace whereof, no jocund health that Denmark drinks today but the great cannon to the clouds shall tell, and the King's rouse the heaven shall bruit again, re-speaking earthly thunder. – Come away.

Exeunt all except Hamlet.

HAMLET: O, that this too too solid flesh would melt, thaw, and resolve itself into a dew! Or that the Everlasting had not fixed His canon 'gainst self-slaughter! O God! O God! How weary, stale, flat, and unprofitable seem to me all the uses of this world! Fie on't! O fie! 'Tis an unweeded garden that grows to seed; things rank and gross in nature possess it merely. That it should come to this! But two months dead! O nay, not so much, not two; so excellent a king; that was, to this, Hyperion to a satyr; so loving to my mother, that he might not beteem the winds of heaven visit her face too roughly. Heaven and earth! Must I remember? Why, she would hang on him, as if increase of appetite had grown by what it fed on: and yet, within a month – let me not think on't –Frailty, thy name is woman! – A little month, or ere those shoes were old with which she followed my poor father's body, like Niobe, all tears: within a month, ere yet the salt of most unrighteous tears had left the flushing in her galled eyes, she married: O, most wicked speed, to post with such dexterity to incestuous sheets!

It is not, nor it cannot come to good: but break, my heart, for
I must hold my tongue!

Enter Horatio, Marcellus, and Bernardo.

HORATIO: Hail to your lordship!

HAMLET: I am glad to see you well: Horatio – or do I forget myself.

HORATIO: The same, my lord, and your poor servant ever.

HAMLET: Sir, my good friend; I'll change that name with you: and what
make you from Wittenberg, Horatio? – Marcellus.

MARCELLUS: My good lord.

HAMLET: I am very glad to see you. (*To Bernardo*) Good even, sir.
– But what, in faith, make you from Wittenberg?

HORATIO: A truant disposition, my good lord.

HAMLET: I would not hear your enemy say so: I know you are no
truant. But what is your affair in Elsinore? We'll teach you to
drink deep ere you depart.

HORATIO: My lord, I came to see your father's funeral.

HAMLET: I pray thee, do not mock me, fellow student; I think it was to
see my mother's wedding.

HORATIO: Indeed, my lord, it followed hard upon.

HAMLET: Thrift, thrift, Horatio! The funeral baked meats did coldly
furnish forth the marriage tables. Would I had met my dearest
foe in heaven ere I had ever seen that day, Horatio! – My father,
– methinks I see my father.

HORATIO: O, where, my lord?

HAMLET: In my mind's eye, Horatio.

HORATIO: I saw him once; he was a goodly king.

HAMLET: He was a man, take him for all in all, I shall not look upon his
like again.

HORATIO: My lord, I think I saw him yesternight.

HAMLET: Saw who?

HORATIO: My lord, the King your father.

HAMLET: The King, my father! For God's love, let me hear.

HORATIO: Two nights together had these gentlemen, Marcellus and Bernardo, on their watch, in the dead waste and middle of the night, been thus encountered. A figure like your father, appears before them, and with solemn march goes slow and stately by them. This to me in dreadful secrecy impart they did; and I with them the third night kept the watch: where, as they had delivered, both in time, form of the thing, each word made true and good, the apparition comes: I knew your father; these hands are not more like.

HAMLET: But where was this?

HORATIO: My lord, upon the platform where we watched.

HAMLET: Did you not speak to it?

HORATIO: My lord, I did; but answer made it none: yet once, methought, it lifted up its head, and did address itself to motion, like as it would speak: but even then, the morning cock crew loud; and at the sound it shrunk in haste away, and vanished from our sight.

HAMLET: 'Tis very strange.

HORATIO: As I do live, my honour'd lord, 'tis true; and we did think it writ down in our duty to let you know of it.

HAMLET: Indeed, indeed, sirs, but this troubles me. Hold you the watch tonight?

MARCELLUS, BERNARDO: We do my lord.

HAMLET: Looked he frowningly?

HORATIO: A countenance more in sorrow than in anger.

HAMLET: Pale or red?

HORATIO: Nay, very pale.

HAMLET: And fixed his eyes upon you?

HORATIO: Most constantly.

HAMLET: I would I had been there.

HORATIO: It would have much amazed you.

HAMLET: Very like, very like. Stayed it long?

HORATIO: While one with moderate haste might tell a hundred.

MARCELLUS, BERNARDO: Longer, longer.

HORATIO: Not when I saw it.

HAMLET: His beard was grizzled? No?

HORATIO: It was, as I have seen it in his life, a sable silvered.

HAMLET: I will watch tonight; perchance 'twill walk again.

HORATIO: I warrant it will.

HAMLET: If it assume my noble father's person, I'll speak to it, though
hell itself should gape, and bid me hold my peace. I pray you
all, if you hath hitherto concealed this sight, let it be tenable
in your silence still. I will requite your loves. So, fare you well:
upon the platform 'twixt eleven and twelve, I'll visit you.

ALL: Our duty to your honour.

HAMLET: Your loves, as mine to you: farewell.

Exeunt Horatio, Marcellus, and Bernardo.

HAMLET: My father's spirit in arms! All is not well. I doubt some foul
play; would the night were come! Till then sit still, my soul:
foul deeds will rise, though all the earth o'erwhelm them to
men's eyes.

Exit.

SCENE 3 'FIRST POLONIUS'S HOUSE'

A room in Polonius's house. Enter Laertes and Ophelia.

LAERTES: My necessaries are embarked: farewell! And, sister, do not
sleep, but let me hear from you.

OPHELIA: Do you doubt that?

LAERTES: For Hamlet, and the trifling of his favour, hold it a fashion,
and a toy in blood; no more.

OPHELIA: No more but so?

LAERTES: Think it no more: fear it, Ophelia, fear it, my dear sister;
and keep you in the rear of your affection, out of the shot and
danger of desire. Be wary, then: best safety lies in fear: youth
to itself rebels, though none else near.

OPHELIA: I shall the effect of this good lesson keep as watchman to
my heart.

Enter Polonius.

LAERTES: A double blessing is a double grace; occasion smiles upon a
second leave.

POLONIUS: Yet here, Laertes? Aboard, aboard, for shame!

Lays his hand on Laertes' head.

There – my blessing with you![2] And these few precepts in my
memory look thou character. Give thy thoughts no tongue,
nor any unproportioned thought his act. Be thou familiar,
but by no means vulgar. The friends thou hast, and their
adoption tried, grapple them to thy soul with hoops of steel;
but do not dull thy palm with entertainment of each new-
hatched, unfledged comrade. Beware of entrance to a quarrel;
but, being in, bear't that the opposed may beware of thee.

---

2   Originally 'thee'.

Give every man thine ear, but few thy voice. Take each man's censure but reserve thy judgement. Costly thy habit as thy purse can buy, but not expressed in fancy; rich, not gaudy: for the apparel oft proclaims the man. Neither a borrower, nor a lender be: for loan oft loses both itself and friend; and borrowing dulls the edge of husbandry. This above all – to thine ownself be true, and it must follow, as the night the day, thou canst not then be false to any man. Farewell: my blessing season this in thee!

LAERTES: Farewell, Ophelia; and remember well what I have said to you.

OPHELIA: 'Tis in my memory locked, and you yourself shall keep the key of it.

LAERTES: Farewell.

Exit Laertes.

POLONIUS: What is't, Ophelia, he hath said to you?

OPHELIA: So please you, something touching the Lord Hamlet.

POLONIUS: Marry, well bethought! 'Tis told me, he hath very oft of late given private time to you; and you yourself have of your audience been most free and bounteous: if it be so (as so 'tis put to me, and that in way of caution), I must tell you, you do not understand yourself so clearly, as it behoves my daughter, and your honour. What is between you? Give me up the truth.

OPHELIA: He hath, my lord, of late made many tenders of his affection to me.

POLONIUS: Affection, pooh! You speak like a green girl. Do you believe his tenders, as you call them?

OPHELIA: I do not know, my lord, what I should think.

POLONIUS: Marry, I'll teach you: think yourself a baby; that you have ta'en these tenders for true pay.

OPHELIA: My lord, he hath importuned me with love, in honourable
     fashion.

POLONIUS: Ay, fashion you may call it; go to, go to.

OPHELIA: And hath given countenance to his speech, my lord, with
     almost all the holy vows of heaven.

POLONIUS: Ay, springes to catch woodcocks. I do know, when the blood
     burns, how prodigal the soul lends the tongue vows: from this
     time be somewhat scanter of your maiden presence; set your
     entreatments at a higher rate than a command to parley. This is
     for all – I would not in plain terms, from this time forth, have
     you so slander any moment's leisure, as to give word or talk
     with the Lord Hamlet. Look to't, I charge you; come your ways.

OPHELIA: I shall obey, my lord.

     Exeunt.

SCENE 4 'SECOND BATTLEMENT'

The battlements. Enter Hamlet, Horatio, and Marcellus.

HAMLET: The air bites shrewdly; it is very cold.

HORATIO: It is a nipping and an eager air.

HAMLET: What hour now?

HORATIO: I think it lacks of twelve.

MARCELLUS: No, it is struck.

HORATIO: Indeed? I heard it not: then it draws near the season
     wherein the spirit held his wont to walk.

     A noise and ordnance shot off within.

     What does that mean my lord?

HAMLET: The King doth wake tonight and takes his rouse, keeps
     wassail, and the swaggering up-spring reels; and, as he drains

his draughts of Rhenish down, the kettle-drum and trumpet thus bray out the triumph of his pledge.

HORATIO: Is it a custom?

HAMLET: Ay, marry, is't: but to my mind, though I am native here, and to the manner born, it is a custom more honoured in the breach than the observance.

Enter Ghost.

HORATIO: Look, my lord, it comes!

HAMLET: Angels and ministers of grace, defend us! Be thou a spirit of health, or goblin damned, bring with thee airs from heaven, or blasts from hell, be thy intents wicked or charitable, thou com'st in such a questionable shape, that I will speak to thee. What may this mean, that thou, dead corpse, revisit'st thus the glimpses of the moon, making night hideous. Say, why is this? Wherefore? What should we do?

The Ghost beckons Hamlet.

HORATIO: It beckons you go away with it.

MARCELLUS: But do not go with it.

HORATIO: No, by no means.

HAMLET: It will not speak: then I will follow it.

HORATIO: Do not, my lord.

HAMLET: Why, what should be the fear? It waves me still. Go on; I'll follow thee.

MARCELLUS: You shall not go, my lord.

HAMLET: Hold off your hands.

HORATIO: Be ruled: you shall not go.

HAMLET: My fate cries out, and makes each petty artery in this body as hardy as the Nemean lion's nerve.

Ghost beckons.

Still am I called: unhand me, gentlemen.

Breaking from them.

By heaven, I'll make a ghost of him that lets me: I say, away!

Go on; I'll follow thee.

Exeunt Ghost and Hamlet. Exeunt Horatio and Marcellus.

SCENE 5 'GHOST'

Another part of the battlements.

HAMLET: Whither wilt thou lead me? Speak: I'll go no further.

GHOST: Mark me.

HAMLET: I will.

GHOST: My hour is almost come, when I to sulphurous and tormenting
flames must render up myself.

HAMLET: Alas, poor ghost!

GHOST: Pity me not; but lend thy serious hearing to what I shall unfold.

HAMLET: Speak: I am bound to hear.

GHOST: So art thou to revenge, when thou shalt hear.

HAMLET: What?

GHOST: I am thy father's spirit, doomed for a certain term to walk
the night, and, for the day, confined to fast in fires, till the foul
crimes, done in my days of nature, are burnt and purged away.
But that I am forbid to tell the secrets of my prison-house,
I could a tale unfold, whose lightest word would harrow up thy
soul. List, O list! If thou didst ever thy dear father love –

HAMLET: O God!

GHOST: Revenge his foul and most unnatural murder.

HAMLET: Murder?

GHOST: Murder most foul, as in the best it is; but this most foul, strange, and unnatural.

HAMLET: Haste me to know it, that I, with wings as swift as meditation, or the thoughts of love, may sweep to my revenge.

GHOST: I find thee apt. Now, Hamlet, hear: 'tis given out that, sleeping in mine orchard, a serpent stung me: so the whole ear of Denmark is by a forged process of my death rankly abused: but know, thou noble youth, the serpent that did sting thy father's life now wears his crown.

HAMLET: O my prophetic soul! My uncle!

GHOST: Ay, that incestuous, that adulterous beast, with witchcraft of his wit, with traitorous gifts, won his shameful lust the will of my most seeming virtuous queen. O Hamlet, what a falling off was there! But virtue, as it never will be moved, though lewdness court it in a shape of heaven, so lust, though to a radiant angel linked,[3] will sate itself in a celestial bed and prey on garbage. But soft! Methinks I scent the morning air; brief let me be. Sleeping within my orchard, my custom always in the afternoon, upon my secure hour thy uncle stole, with juice of cursed hebenon in a vial, and in the porches of my ears did pour the leperous distilment: thus was I, sleeping, by a brother's hand, of life, of crown, of queen, at once despatched. If thou hast nature in thee, bear it not; let not the royal bed of Denmark be a couch for luxury and damned incest. But, howsoever thou pursu'st this act, taint not thy mind, nor let thy soul contrive against thy mother aught. Fare thee well at once! The glow-worm shows the matin to be near, and 'gins to pale his uneffectual fire. Adieu, adieu! Hamlet, remember me.

Exit.

---

3   Phrase added in pencil.

HAMLET: O all you host of heaven! Remember thee? Ay, thou poor
ghost, while memory holds a seat in this distracted globe.
Remember thee? Yes, from the table of my memory, I'll wipe
away all trivial fond records, that youth and observation
copied there; and thy commandment all alone shall live within
the book and volume of my brain, unmixed with baser matter.
Yes, by heaven! O most pernicious woman! O villain, villain,
smiling , damned villain! Now to my word: it is 'Adieu, adieu!
remember me'. I have sworn't.

HORATIO: (*Within*) My lord!, my lord!

MARCELLUS: (*Within*) Lord Hamlet!

HORATIO: (*Within*) Heaven secure him!

Enter Horatio and Marcellus.

MARCELLUS: How is't, my noble lord?

HORATIO: What news, my lord?

HAMLET: O, wonderful!

HORATIO: Good my lord, tell it.

HAMLET: No; you'll reveal it.

HORATIO: Not I, my lord, by heaven.

MARCELLUS: Nor I, my lord.

HAMLET: How say you, then; would heart of man once think it?
– But you'll be secret?

HORATIO AND MARCELLUS: Ay, by heaven, my lord.

HAMLET: There's ne'er a villain dwelling in all Denmark but he's an
arrant knave.

HORATIO: There needs no ghost, my lord, come from the grave to tell
us this.

HAMLET: Why, right, you are i' the right; and so, without more
circumstance at all, I hold it fit that we shake hands and part:

you, as your business and desire shall point you; for every man
hath business and desire, such as it is; and for mine own poor
part, look you, I'll go pray.

HORATIO: These are but wild and whirling words, my lord.

HAMLET: I am sorry to offend you, heartily; yes, faith, heartily.

HORATIO: There is no offence, my lord.

HAMLET: Yes, by Saint Patrick, but there is, Horatio, and much offence
too. Touching this vision here, it is an honest ghost, that let
me tell you: for your desire to know what is between us,
o'ermaster it as you may. And now, good friends, as you are
friends, scholars, and soldiers, give me one poor request.

HORATIO: What is't, my lord? We will.

HAMLET: Never make it known what you have seen tonight.

HORATIO and MARCELLUS: My lord, we will not.

HAMLET: Nay, but swear't.

HORATIO: In faith, my lord, not I.

MARCELLUS: Nor I, my lord, in faith.

HAMLET: Upon my sword.

MARCELLUS: We have sworn, my lord, already.

HAMLET: Indeed, upon my sword, indeed.

HORATIO: Propose the oath, my lord.

HAMLET: Never [to] speak of this that you have seen, swear by
my sword.

HORATIO: O day and night, but this is wondrous strange!

HAMLET: And therefore as a stranger give it welcome. There are
more things in heaven and earth, Horatio, than are dreamt
of in your philosophy. But come: here, as before, never, so
help you mercy, how strange or odd soe'er I bear myself –
as I, perchance, hereafter shall think meet to put an antic

disposition on – that you, at such times seeing me, never shall note that you know aught of me – this not to do, so grace and mercy at your most need help you, swear. Rest, rest, perturbed spirit! – So, gentlemen, with all my love I do commend me to you: and what so poor a man as Hamlet is may do, to express his love and friending to you, God willing, shall not lack. Let us go in together: and still your fingers on your lips, I pray. The time is out of joint: O cursed spite, that ever I was born to set it right! Nay, come, let's go together.

SCENE 6 'SECOND POLONIUS'S HOUSE'

A room in Polonius's house. Enter Polonius and Reynaldo.

POLONIUS: Give my son this money and these notes, Reynaldo.

REYNALDO: I will, my lord.

POLONIUS: You shall do marvellous wisely, good Reynaldo, before you visit him, to make inquiry of his behaviour.

REYNALDO: My lord, I did intend it.

POLONIUS: Observe his inclination in yourself.

REYNALDO: I shall, my lord.

POLONIUS: And let him ply his music.

REYNALDO: Well, my lord.

POLONIUS: Farewell.

Exit Reynaldo. Enter Ophelia.

How now, Ophelia! what's the matter?

OPHELIA: Alas, my lord, I have been so affrighted!

POLONIUS: With what in in the name of God?

OPHELIA: My lord, as I was sewing in my chamber, Lord Hamlet, with a look so piteous in purport, as if he had been loosed out of hell to speak of horrors – he comes before me.

POLONIUS: Mad for thy love?

OPHELIA: My lord, I do not know; but truly, I do fear it.

POLONIUS: What said he?

OPHELIA: He took me by the wrist, and held me hard, then goes he to the length of all his arm; and, with his other hand thus o'er his brow, he falls to such perusal of my face, as he would draw it. Long stayed he so; at last, a little shaking of mine arm, he raised a sigh so piteous and profound, that it did seem to shatter all his bulk, and end his being; that done he lets me go: and, with his head over his shoulder turned, he seemed to find his way without his eyes; for out of doors he went without their help, and, to the last, bended their light on me.

POLONIUS: Come, go with me: I will go seek the King. This is the very ecstasy of love; I am sorry. What, have you given him any hard words of late?

OPHELIA: No, my good lord; but, as you did command, I did repel his letters, and denied his access to me.

POLONIUS: That hath made him mad. I am sorry that with better heed and judgement I had not quoted him: I feared he did but trifle, and meant to wreck thee. Come, go we to the King: this must be known.

SCENE 7 'WELCOME ROSENCRANTZ and GUILDENSTERN'

The Council Chamber. Enter King, Queen, Rosencrantz, Guildenstern, and Attendants.

KING: Welcome, dear Rosencrantz and Guildenstern! Moreover that we did long to see you, the need we have to use you did provoke our hasty sending. Something have you heard of Hamlet's transformation; so I call it, since nor the exterior nor the inward man resembles that it was. What it should be, more than his father's death, that thus hath put him so much from the understanding of himself, I cannot dream of: I entreat you both, so by your companies to draw him on to pleasures, and to gather, so much as from occasion you may glean, whether aught, to us unknown, afflicts him thus, that, opened, lies within our remedy.

QUEEN: Good gentlemen, he hath much talked of you: and sure I am two men there are not living to whom he more adheres. If it will please you to show us so much gentry and good will as to expend your time with us awhile, for the supply and profit of our hope, your visitation shall receive such thanks as fits a king's remembrance.

ROSENCRANTZ: Both your majesties might, by the sovereign power you have of us, put your dread pleasure more into command than to entreaty.

GUILDENSTERN: But we both obey, and here give up ourselves, in the full bent, to lay our services freely at your feet, and be commanded.

QUEEN: And I beseech you instantly to visit my too much changed son.

GUILDENSTERN: Heavens make our presence and our practices pleasant and helpful to him!

QUEEN: Ay, amen!

Exeunt Rosencrantz, Guildenstern, and Attendants. Enter Polonius.

POLONIUS: The ambassadors from Norway, my good lord, are joyfully returned.

KING: Thou still hast been the father of good news.

POLONIUS: Have I, my lord? I assure you, my good liege, I hold my duty, as I hold my soul, both to my God, and to my gracious King; and I do think (or else this brain of mine hunts not the trail of policy so sure as it hath used to do), that I have found the very cause of Hamlet's lunacy.

KING: O, speak of that; that do I long to hear. He tells me, my dear Gertrude, he hath found the head and source of all your son's distemper.

POLONIUS: My liege, and madam, to expostulate what majesty should be, what duty is, why day is day, night night, and time is time, were nothing but to waste day, night, time.[4] Therefore, since brevity is the soul of wit, and tediousness the limbs and outward flourishes, I will be brief: your noble son is mad; mad I call it, for, to define true madness, what is't but to be nothing else but mad? But let that go.

QUEEN: More matter, with less art.

POLONIUS: Madam, I swear I use no art at all. That he is mad, 'tis true; 'tis true 'tis pity; and pity 'tis 'tis true: a foolish figure; but farewell it, for I will use no art. Mad let us grant him then: and now remains that we find out the cause of this effect – or rather

---

4   Final phrase added in pencil.

say, the cause of this defect, for this effect defective comes by cause; thus it remains and the remainder thus. Perpend. I have a daughter – have while she is mine – who, in her duty and obedience, mark, hath given me this: now gather and surmise.

He reads a letter.

'To the celestial, and my soul's idol, the most beautiful Ophelia'
– that's a vile phrase.
'Doubt thou the stars of fire;
Doubt that the sun doth move;
Doubt truth to be a liar;
But never doubt I love.
O dear Ophelia, I am ill at these numbers: I have not art to reckon my groans: but that I love thee best, O most best, believe it. Adieu.
Thine evermore, most dear lady,
Whilst this machine is to him,
Hamlet.'
This in obedience hath my daughter shown me.

KING: But how hath she received his love?

POLONIUS: What do you think of me?

KING: As a man faithful and honourable.

POLONIUS: I would fain prove so. But what might you think, when I had seen this hot love on the wing (as I perceived it, I must tell you that, before my daughter told me), what might you, or my dear majesty your queen here, think, if I had looked upon this love with idle sight; what might you think? No, I went round to work, and my young mistress thus I did bespeak: 'Lord Hamlet is a prince out of thy sphere;[5] this must not be'. And then I precepts

---

5   'Star' in some editions.

gave her, that she should lock herself from his resort, which done, she took the fruits of my advice: and he, repulsed (a short tale to make), fell into a sadness; then into a fast; thence to a watch; thence into a weakness; thence to a lightness; and by this declension into the madness wherein he now raves, and all we mourn for.

KING: Do you think 'tis this?

QUEEN: It may be, very likely.

POLONIUS: Hath there been a time (I'd fain know that), that I have positively said, ''Tis so', when it proved otherwise?

KING: Not that I know.

POLONIUS: If circumstances lead me, I will find where the truth is hid.

KING: How may we try it further?

POLONIUS: You know, sometimes he walks for hours together here in the lobby.

QUEEN: So he does indeed.

POLONIUS: At such a time I'll loose my daughter to him: be you and I behind an arras then; mark the encounter; if he love her not, and be not from his reason fallen thereon, let me be no assistant for a state, but keep a farm and carters.

KING: We will try it.

Enter Hamlet, reading.

QUEEN: But look, where sadly the poor wretch comes reading.

POLONIUS: Away, I did beseech you, both away: I'll board him presently: O, give me leave.

Exeunt King, Queen, and Attendants.

How does my good lord Hamlet?

HAMLET: Well, God-a-mercy.

POLONIUS: Do you know me, my lord?

HAMLET: Excellent well; you are a fishmonger.

POLONIUS: Not I, my lord.

HAMLET: Then I would you were so honest a man.

POLONIUS: Honest, my lord?

HAMLET: Ay, sir, to be honest, as this world goes, is to be one man picked out of ten thousand.

POLONIUS: That's very true, my lord.

HAMLET: Have you a daughter?

POLONIUS: I have, my lord!

HAMLET: Let her not walk i' the sun: conception is a blessing; but not as your daughter may conceive: – friend, look to't.

POLONIUS: How say you by that? – (*Aside*) Still harping on my daughter: yet he knew me not at first; he said I was a fishmonger; he is far gone, far gone: and truly in my youth I suffered much extremity for love; very near this. I'll speak to him again. – What do you read, my lord?

HAMLET: Words, words, words.

POLONIUS: What is the matter, my lord?

HAMLET: Between who?

POLONIUS: I mean, the matter you read, my lord.

HAMLET: Slanders, sir: for the satirical rogue says here that old men have grey beards; that their faces are wrinkled; and that they have a plentiful lack of wit, together with most weak hams: all of which, sir, I hold it not honesty to have it thus set down; for you yourself, sir, should be old as I am, if like a crab, you could go backward.

POLONIUS: (*Aside*) Though this be madness, yet there is method in it.

– Will you walk out of the air, my lord?

HAMLET: Into my grave?

POLONIUS: Indeed, that is out o' the air. (*Aside*) – How pregnant
sometimes his replies are! My honourable lord, I will most
humbly take my leave of you.

HAMLET: You cannot, sir, take from me anything that I will more
willingly part withal; except my life, except my life, except my life.

POLONIUS: Fare you well, my lord.

HAMLET: These tedious old fools!

Enter Rosencrantz and Guildenstern.

POLONIUS: You do to seek the Lord Hamlet; there he is.

ROSENCRANTZ: (*To Polonius*) God save you, sir!

Exit Polonius.

GUILDENSTERN: Mine honoured lord!

ROSENCRANTZ: My most dear lord!

HAMLET: My excellent good friends! How dost thou Guildenstern?
Ah, Rosencrantz! Good lads, how do ye both?

ROSENCRANTZ: As the indifferent children of the earth.

GUILDENSTERN: Happy in that we are not over happy.

HAMLET: What's the news?

ROSENCRANTZ: None, my lord, but that the world's grown honest.

HAMLET: Then is doomsday near: but what have you, my good friends,
deserved at the hands of Fortune, that she sends you to prison
hither?

GUILDENSTERN: Prison, my lord?

HAMLET: Denmark's a prison.

ROSENCRANTZ: Then is the world one.

HAMLET: A goodly one; in which there are many confines, wards,
and dungeons, Denmark being one of the worst.

ROSENCRANTZ: We think not so, my lord.

HAMLET: Why, then, 'tis none to you; for there is nothing either good
or bad, but thinking makes it so: to me it is a prison.

ROSENCRANTZ: Why, then, your ambition makes it one; 'tis too narrow
for your mind.

HAMLET: O God! I could be bounded in a nutshell and count myself a
king of infinite space, were it not that I have bad dreams. But, in
the beaten way of friendship, what make you at Elsinore?

ROSENCRANTZ: To visit you, my lord; no other occasion.

HAMLET: Beggar that I am, I am even poor in thanks, but I thank you.[6]
Were you not sent for? Is it your own inclining? Is it a free
visitation? Come, deal justly with me: come, come; nay, speak.

GUILDENSTERN: What should we say, my lord?

HAMLET: Why, anything – but to the purpose. You were sent for, and
there is a kind of confession in your looks, which your modesties
have not craft enough to colour; I know the good King and
Queen have sent for you. Be even and direct with me, whether
you were sent for, or no.

ROSENCRANTZ: (*Aside to Guildenstern*) What say you?

GUILDENSTERN: My lord, we were sent for.

HAMLET: I will tell you why: I have of late (but wherefore I know not)
lost all my mirth, forgone all custom of exercises; and, indeed,
it goes so heavily with my disposition, man delights not me; no,
nor woman either, though, by your smiling, you seem to say so.

ROSENCRANTZ: My lord, there was no such stuff in my thoughts

HAMLET: Why did you laugh, then, when I said 'man delights not me'?

ROSENCRANTZ: To think, my lord, if you delight not in man, what lenten
entertainment the players shall receive from you: we met[7] them
on the way; and hither are they come to offer you service.

---

6   Line added in pencil.
7   Originally 'coted'.

HAMLET: He that plays the King shall be welcome. – What players are they?

ROSENCRANTZ: Even those you were wont to take delight in, the tragedians of the city. (*Noise within.*)

GUILDENSTERN: There are the players.

HAMLET: Gentlemen, you are welcome to Elsinore. You are welcome: but my uncle-father and aunt-mother are deceived.

GUILDENSTERN: In what, my dear lord?

HAMLET: I am but mad north-north-west: when the wind is southerly, I know a hawk from a handsaw.

Enter Polonius.

POLONIUS: Well be with you, gentlemen.

HAMLET: Hark you, Guildenstern – and you too – that great baby you see there is not yet out of his swathing-clouts. I will prophesy he comes to tell me of the players: mark it. – You say right, sir: o' Monday morning, 'twas so indeed.

POLONIUS: My lord, I have news to tell you.

HAMLET: My lord, I have news to tell you. When Roscius was an actor in Rome –

POLONIUS: The actors are come hither, my lord.

HAMLET: Buzz, buzz!

POLONIUS: Upon my honour, the best actors in the world, either for tragedy, comedy, history, pastoral, pastoral-comical, historical-pastoral, tragical-historical, tragical-comical-historical-pastoral, scene individable, or poem unlimited: these are the only men.

HAMLET: O Jephthah, judge of Israel, what a treasure hadst thou!

POLONIUS: What a treasure had he, my lord?

HAMLET: Why,

'One fair daughter, and no more,

The which he loved passing well.'[8]

POLONIUS: (*Aside*) Still on my daughter.

HAMLET: Am I not i' the right, old Jephthah?

POLONIUS: If you call me Jephthah, my lord, I have a daughter that
I love passing well.

HAMLET: Nay, that follows not. For look, where my abridgement comes.

Enter four or five Players.

You are welcome, masters; welcome all: – I am glad to see thee well: –
welcome, good friends. – Good my lord, will you see the players
well bestowed? Do you hear, let them be well used; for they are
the abstracts and brief chronicles of the time: after your death
you were better have a bad epitaph than their ill report while
you live.

POLONIUS: My lord, I will use them according to their desert.

HAMLET: God's bodykins, man, much better: use every man after his
desert and who should 'scape whipping? Use them after your
own honour and dignity: the less they deserve, the more merit is
in your bounty. Take them in.

POLONIUS: Come, sirs.

HAMLET: Follow him, friends: we'll hear a play tomorrow.

Exit Polonius, with all the Players except the first.

Dost thou hear me, old friend: can you play *The Murder of Gonzago?*

FIRST PLAYER: Ay, my lord.

HAMLET: We'll have it to-morrow night. You could, for a need, study a
speech of some dozen or sixteen lines, which I would set down
and insert in't, could you not?

FIRST PLAYER: Ay, my lord.

---

8   Quote from an unidentified ballad.

HAMLET: Very well. – Follow that lord, and look you mock him not.

   Exit First Player.

     (To Rosencrantz and Guildenstern) My good friends, I'll leave you till night. You are welcome to Elsinore.

ROSENCRANTZ: Good my lord.

   Exeunt Rosencrantz and Guildenstern.

HAMLET: Ay, so, God be wi' you! – Now I am alone. O, what a rogue and peasant slave am I! Am I a coward? Who calls me villain? Breaks my pate across? Tweaks me by the nose? Gives me the lie i' the throat, as deep as to the lungs? Who does me this, ha? Why, I should take it, for it cannot be but I am pigeon-livered and lack gall to make oppression bitter; or, ere this, I should have fatted all the region kites with this slave's offal: bloody, bawdy villain! Remorseless, treacherous, lecherous, kindless villain! O, vengeance! Why, what an ass am I! This is most brave, that I, the son of a dear father murdered, prompted to my revenge by heaven and hell, must, like a whore, unpack my heart with words, and fall a-cursing, like a very drab, a scullion! Fie upon't! Foh! About, my brain! I have heard that guilty creatures sitting at a play have by the very cunning of the scene been struck so to the soul that presently they have proclaimed their malefactions; for murder, though it have no tongue, will speak with most miraculous organ. I'll have these players play something like the murder of my father before mine uncle: I'll observe his looks; I'll tent him to the quick: if he but blench, I know my course. The spirit that I have seen may be the devil: and the devil hath power to assume a pleasing shape; yea, and perhaps out of my weakness, and my melancholy (as he is very potent with such spirits), abuses me to damn me: I'll have grounds more relative than this: the play's the thing wherein I'll catch the conscience of the King.

Exit.

SCENE 8 'NUNNERY'

A room in the castle. Enter King, Queen, Polonius, Rosencrantz and Guildenstern.

KING: And can you, by no drift of circumstance, get from him why he puts on this confusion, grating so harshly all his days of quiet with turbulent and dangerous lunacy?

ROSENCRANTZ: He does confess he feels himself distracted; but for what cause, he will by no means speak.

QUEEN: Did he receive you well?

ROSENCRANTZ: Most like a gentleman.

QUEEN: Did you assay him to any pastime?

ROSENCRANTZ: Madam, it so fell out, that certain players we o'er-raught on the way; of these we told him: and there did seem in him a kind of joy to hear of it: they are about the court; and, as I think, they have already order this night to play before him.

POLONIUS: 'Tis most true: and he beseeched me to entreat your majesties to hear and see the matter.

KING: With all my heart: and it doth much content me to hear him so inclined. Good gentlemen, give him a further edge, and drive his purpose on to these delights.

ROSENCRANTZ: We shall, my lord.

Exeunt Rosencrantz and Guildenstern.

KING: Sweet Gertrude, leave us too; for we have closely sent for Hamlet hither, that he, as 'twere by accident, may here affront Ophelia:

her father and myself (lawful espials), will so bestow ourselves
that, seeing unseen, we may of their encounter frankly judge;
if't be the affliction of his love, or no, that thus he suffers for.

QUEEN: I shall obey you. And for your part, Ophelia, I do wish that your
good beauties be the happy cause of Hamlet's wildness: so shall
I hope your virtues will bring him to his wonted way again, to
both your honours.

OPHELIA: Madam, I wish it may.

Exit Queen.

POLONIUS: Ophelia, walk you here. – Gracious, so please you, we will
bestow ourselves. – Read on this book; that show of such an
exercise may colour your loneliness. I hear him coming; let's
withdraw, my lord.

Exeunt King and Polonius.

HAMLET: To be, or not to be – that is the question: whether 'tis nobler in
the mind to suffer the slings and arrows of outrageous fortune,
or to take arms against a sea of troubles, and by opposing end
them? To die – to sleep – no more; and by a sleep, to say we end
the heartache and the thousand natural shocks that flesh is
heir to – 'tis a consummation devoutly to be wished. To die – to
sleep – to sleep, perchance to dream – ay, there's the rub; for
in that sleep of death what dreams may come, when we have
shuffled off this mortal coil, must give us pause. There's the
respect that makes calamity of so long life: for who would bear
the whips and scorns of time, the oppressor's wrong, the proud
man's contumely, the pangs of despised love, the law's delay,
the insolence of office, and the spurns that patient merit of the
unworthy takes, when he himself might his quietus make with a
bare bodkin? Who would fardels bear, to grunt and sweat under

a weary life, but that the dread of something after death, the undiscovered country, from whose bourn no traveller returns, puzzles the will, and makes us rather bear those ills we have than fly to others that we know not of? Thus conscience does make cowards of us all; and thus the native hue of resolution is sicklied o'er with the pale cast of thought: and enterprises of great pitch and moment, with this regard, their currents turn awry, and lose the name of action. – Soft you now, the fair Ophelia! – Nymph, in thy orisons be all my sins remembered?[9]

OPHELIA: Good my lord, how does your honour for this many a day?

HAMLET: I humbly thank you; well, well, well.

OPHELIA: My lord, I have remembrances of yours, that I have longed long to redeliver; I pray you, now receive them.

HAMLET: No, not I; I never gave you aught.

OPHELIA: My honoured lord, I know right well you did; and with them words of so sweet breath composed as made the things more rich: their perfume lost, take these again; for to the noble mind, rich gifts wax poor, when givers prove unkind. There, my lord.

HAMLET: Ha! Are you honest?

OPHELIA: My lord?

HAMLET: Are you fair?

OPHELIA: What means your lordship?

HAMLET: That if you be honest and fair, your honesty should admit no discourse to your beauty.

OPHELIA: Could beauty, my lord, have better commerce than with honesty?

HAMLET: Ay, truly. – I did love you once.

---

9   Originally no question mark at this point.

OPHELIA: Indeed, my lord, you made me believe so.

HAMLET: You should not have believed me – I loved you not.[10]

OPHELIA: I was the more deceived.

HAMLET: Get thee to a nunnery: why wouldst thou be a breeder of sinners? I am myself indifferent honest; but yet I could accuse me of such things that it were better my mother had not borne me. What should such fellows as I do crawling between heaven and earth? We are arrant knaves, all; believe none of us. Go thy ways to a nunnery. Where's your father?

OPHELIA: At home, my lord.

HAMLET: Let the doors be shut upon him, that he may play the fool nowhere but in his own house. Farewell.

OPHELIA: O, help him, you sweet heavens!

HAMLET: If thou dost marry, I'll give you[11] this plague for thy dowry: be thou as chaste as ice, as pure as snow, thou shalt not escape calumny. Get thee to a nunnery, go: farewell. Or, if you[12] wilt needs marry, marry a fool; for wise men know well enough what monsters you make of them. Go to a nunnery, go; and quickly too. Farewell.

Exit Hamlet.

OPHELIA: O, what a noble mind is here o'erthrown! The courtier's, soldier's, scholar's, eye, tongue, sword; the expectancy and rose of the fair state, the glass of fashion and the mould of form, the observed of all observers, quite, quite down! And I, of ladies most deject and wretched, that suck[13] the honey of his music vows, now see that noble and most sovereign reason, like sweet bells jangled, out of tune and harsh; that unmatched form and

---

10 'Indeed … you not' inserted in pencil.
11 Originally 'thee'.
12 Originally 'thou'.
13 Originally 'sucked'.

feature of blown youth blasted with ecstasy. O woe is me, to have seen what I have seen, see what I see!

Re-enter King and Polonius.

KING: Love![14] His affections do not that way tend; nor what he spake, though it lacked form a little, was not like madness. There's something in his soul o'er which his melancholy sits on brood; and, I do doubt, the hatch, and the disclose will be some danger: which, for to prevent, I have, in quick determination, thus set it down: he shall with speed to England for the demand of our neglected tribute. What think you on it?

POLONIUS: It shall do well: but yet I do believe the origin and commencement of his grief sprung from neglected love. How now, Ophelia! You need not tell us what Lord Hamlet said; we heard it all. My lord, do as you please; but, if you hold it fit, after the play let his queen mother all alone entreat him to show his grief: let her be round with him; and I'll be placed, so please you, in the ear of all their conference. If she find him not, to England send him; or confine him where your wisdom best shall think.

KING: It shall be so.

SCENE 9 'PLAY'

The Council Chamber. Enter Hamlet and certain Players.

HAMLET: Speak the speech, I pray you, as I pronounce it to you, trippingly on the tongue: but if you mouth it, as many of your players do, I had as lief the town-crier spoke my lines. Nor do not saw the air too much with your hand, thus; but use all gently: for in the very torrent, tempest, and (as I may say)

---

14 Usually a question mark.

whirlwind of passion, you must acquire and beget a temperance that may give it smoothness.

FIRST PLAYER: I warrant your honour.

HAMLET: Be not too tame neither, but let your own discretion be your tutor: suit the action to the word, the word to the action; with this special observance, that you o'erstep not the modesty of nature: for anything so overdone is from the purpose of playing; whose end, both at the first, and now, was, and is, to hold, as 'twere, the mirror up to nature. O, there be players that I have seen play, and heard others praise, and that highly, that have so strutted and bellowed that I have thought some of Nature's journeymen had made men, and not made them well, they imitated humanity so abominably.

FIRST PLAYER: I hope we have reformed that indifferently with us, sir.

HAMLET: O reform it altogether. And let those that play your clowns speak no more than is set down for them; for there be of them that will themselves laugh to set on some quantity of barren spectators to laugh too; that's villainous, and shows a most pitiful ambition in the fool that uses it. Go, make you ready.

Exeunt Players. Enter Polonius, Rosencrantz and Guildenstern.

How now, my lord! will the King hear this piece of work?

POLONIUS: And the Queen too, and that presently.

HAMLET: Bid the players make haste.

Exit Polonius.

Will you two help to hasten them?

ROSENCRANTZ AND GUILDENSTERN: We will, my lord.

Exeunt Rosencrantz and Guildenstern.

HAMLET: Horatio!

Enter Horatio.

HORATIO: Here, sweet lord, at your service.

HAMLET: Horatio, thou art e'en as just a man as e'er my conversation
coped withal.

HORATIO: O my dear lord –

HAMLET: Nay, do not think I flatter: since my dear soul was mistress of
her choice, and I could of men distinguish, her election [hath]
sealed thee for herself. – There is a play to-night before the King;
one scene of it comes near the circumstance which I have told
thee, of my father's death: I prithee, when thou seest that act
afoot, even with the very comment of thy soul observe mine
uncle: If his occulted guilt do not itself unkennel in one speech,
it is a damned ghost that we have seen, and my imaginations are
as foul as Vulcan's stithy. Give him heedful note.

HORATIO: Well, my lord; if he steal aught the whilst this play is playing,
and 'scape detecting, I will pay the theft.

HAMLET: They are coming to the play; I must be idle; get you a place.

March. Enter King, Queen, Polonius, Ophelia, Rosencrantz,
Guildenstern, and Court.

KING: How fares our cousin Hamlet?

HAMLET: Excellent, i'faith, of the chameleon's dish: I eat the air,
promise-crammed: You cannot feed capons so.

KING: I have nothing with this answer, Hamlet; these words are
not mine.

HAMLET: No, nor mine now. (*To Polonius*) My lord, you played once
in the university, you say?

POLONIUS: That did I, my lord, and was accounted a good actor.

HAMLET: And what did you enact?

POLONIUS: I did enact Julius Caesar; I was killed in the Capitol;
Brutus killed me.

HAMLET: It was a brute part of him to kill so capital a calf there.

    – Be the players ready?

ROSENCRANTZ: Ay, my lord, they stay upon your patience.

QUEEN: Come hither, my dear Hamlet, sit by me.

HAMLET: No, good mother, here's metal more attractive.

    Sits at Ophelia's feet.

POLONIUS: (*To the King*) O ho! Do you mark that?

OPHELIA: You are merry, my lord.

HAMLET: Who, I?

OPHELIA: Ay, my lord.

HAMLET: O God! your only jig-maker. What should a man do but be
merry? For look you how cheerfully my mother looks, and my
father died within these two hours.

OPHELIA: Nay, 'tis twice two months, my lord.

HAMLET: So long? Nay, then, let the devil wear black, for I'll have a suit
of sables. O heavens! die two months ago, and not forgotten yet?

    Enter Prologue.

PROLOGUE:

    For us, and for our tragedy,

    Here stooping to your clemency,

    We beg your hearing patiently.

HAMLET: Is this a prologue, or the motto in[15] a ring?

OPHELIA: 'Tis brief, my lord.

HAMLET: As woman's love.

    Enter Player King and Player Queen.

PLAYER KING:

    Full thirty times hath Phoebus' cart gone round

    Neptune's salt wash and Tellus' orbed ground:

---

15   Originally 'posy of'.

> Since love our hearts, and Hymen did our hands,
> Unite commutual in most sacred bands.

PLAYER QUEEN:

> So many journeys may the sun and moon
> Make us again count o'er, ere love be done!
> But, woe is me, you are so sick of late,
> So far from cheer, and from your former state,
> That I distrust you.
> For women's fear and love holds quantity;
> In neither aught, or in extremity.
> Now, what my love is, proof hath made you know;
> And as my love is sized, my fear is so.

PLAYER KING:

> Faith, I must leave thee, love, and shortly too;
> My operant powers their functions leave to do:
> And thou shalt live in this fair world behind,
> Honoured, beloved; and haply, one as kind
> For husband shalt thou –

PLAYER QUEEN:

> So confound the rest!
> Such love must needs be treason in my breast:
> In second husband let me be accursed!
> None wed the second but who killed the first.

HAMLET: (*Aside*) Wormwood, wormwood.

PLAYER KING:

> I do believe you think what now you speak;
> But what we do determine, oft we break.
> So think thou wilt no second husband wed;
> But die thy thoughts, when thy first lord is dead.

PLAYER QUEEN:

> Nor earth to me give food, nor heaven light!
>
> Sport and repose, lock from me day and night!
>
> Both here and hence, pursue me lasting strife,
>
> If, once a widow, ever I be wife!

HAMLET: If she should break it now!

PLAYER KING:

> 'Tis deeply sworn. Sweet, leave me here awhile:
>
> My spirits grow dull, and fain I would beguile
>
> The tedious day with sleep. (*He sleeps.*)

PLAYER QUEEN:

> Sleep rock thy brain,
>
> And never come mischance between us twain! (*Exit.*)

HAMLET: Madam, how like you this play?

QUEEN: The lady doth protest too much, methinks.

HAMLET: O, but she'll keep her word.

KING: Have you heard the argument? Is there no offence in't?

HAMLET: No, no, they do but jest, poison in jest; no offence in the world.

KING: What do you call the play?

HAMLET: *The Mousetrap*. This play is the image of a murder done in
Vienna: Gonzago is the duke's name; his wife, Baptista: you shall
see anon. 'Tis a knavish piece of work, but what of that? Your
majesty, and we that have free souls, it touches us not: let the
galled jade wince, our withers are unwrung.

> *Enter Player Lucianus.*

This is one Lucianus, nephew to the King. Begin, murderer, leave
thy damnable faces, and begin. Come – 'the croaking raven doth
bellow for revenge'.[16]

---

16   A quote from *Richard III*.

PLAYER LUCIANUS:

> Thoughts black, hands apt, drugs fit, and time agreeing,
>
> Confederate season, else no creature seeing;
>
> Thou mixture rank, of midnight weeds collected,
>
> With Hecate's ban thrice blasted, thrice infected,
>
> Thy natural magic and dire property
>
> On wholesome life usurp immediately.

(He pours the poison into the sleeper's ears.)

HAMLET: He poisons him in the garden for his estate. His name's Gonzago. The story is extant, and written in very choice Italian. You shall see anon how the murderer gets the love of Gonzago's wife.

OPHELIA: The King rises.

HAMLET: What, frighted with false fire?

QUEEN: How fares my lord?

POLONIUS: Give o'er the play.

KING: Give me some light: away!

ALL: Lights, lights, lights!

> *Exeunt all but Hamlet and Horatio.*

HAMLET: O good Horatio, I'll take the ghost's word for a thousand pound.[17]

Interval

---

17 Line added in pencil and ink.

ACT II

SCENE 10 'KING'S CLOSET'

The King's Dressing Room. Enter King, Rosencrantz and Guildenstern.

KING: I like him not, nor stands it safe with us to let his madness
rage. Therefore prepare you: I your commission will forthwith
dispatch, and he to England shall along with you.

GUILDENSTERN: We will ourselves provide. Most holy and religious
fear it is to keep those many bodies safe that live and feed upon
your majesty.

ROSENCRANTZ: Never alone did the King sigh, but with a general groan.

KING: Arm you, I pray you, to this speedy voyage; for we will fetters
put upon this fear, which now goes too free-footed.

ROSENCRANTZ AND GUILDENSTERN: We will haste us.

Exeunt. Enter Polonius.

POLONIUS: My lord, he's going to his mother's closet: behind the arras
I'll convey myself, to hear the process. I'll warrant she'll tax
him home: and, as you said, and wisely was it said, 'tis meet
that some more audience than a mother, since Nature makes
them partial, should o'erhear the speech of vantage. Fare you
well, my liege: I'll call upon you ere you go to bed, and tell you
what I know.

KING: Thanks, my dear lord.

Exit Polonius.

O, my offence is rank, it smells to heaven: it hath the primal
eldest curse upon it, a brother's murder! Pray, can I not: and
what's in prayer but this twofold force, to be forestalled ere

we come to fall, or pardoned being down? Then I'll look up; my fault is past. But O, what form of prayer can serve my turn? 'Forgive me my foul murder?' That cannot be, since I am still possessed of those effects for which I did the murder, my crown, mine own ambition, and my queen. O wretched state! O bosom black as death! O limed soul, that, struggling to be free, art more engaged!

Enter Hamlet.

HAMLET: Now might I do it pat, now he is praying: and now I'll do't.

[He draws his sword.]

And so he goes to heaven, and so am I revenged: that would be scanned: a villain kills my father, and for that I, his sole son, do this same villain send to heaven. O, this is hire and salary, not revenge, to take him in the purging of his soul, when he is fit and seasoned for his passage. No! Up, sword, and know thou a more horrid hent: when he is drunk asleep, or in his rage, or in the incestuous pleasure of his bed, at gaming swearing, or some other act[18] that has no relish of salvation in it, then trip him, [that his heels may kick at heaven,] and that his soul may be as damned and black as hell, whereto it goes. My mother stays: this physic but prolongs thy sickly days.

Exit Hamlet.

KING: My words fly up, my thoughts remain below: words without thoughts never to heaven go.

---

18   Originally 'about some act'.

SCENE 11 'QUEEN'S CLOSET'

The Queen's Bedroom. Enter Queen and Polonius.

POLONIUS: He will come straight. Look you lay home to him: tell him
his pranks have been too broad to bear with, and that your
grace hath screened and stood between much heat and him. I'll
silence me e'en here. Pray you, be round with him.

HAMLET: (*Within*) Mother, mother, mother!

QUEEN: I'll warrant you; fear me not. Withdraw, I hear him coming.

Polonius hides behind the arras. Enter Hamlet.

HAMLET: Now, mother, what's the matter?

QUEEN: Hamlet, thou hast thy father much offended.

HAMLET: Mother, you have my father much offended.

QUEEN: Come, come, you answer with an idle tongue.

HAMLET: Go, go, you question with a wicked tongue.

QUEEN: Why, how now, Hamlet?

HAMLET: What's the matter now?

QUEEN: Have you forgot me?

HAMLET: You are the Queen, your husband's brother's wife: and
(would it were not so) you are my mother.

QUEEN: Nay, then I'll set those to you that can speak.

HAMLET: Come, come, and sit you down: you shall not budge, you go
not till I set you up a glass where you may see the inmost part
of you.

QUEEN: What wilt thou do? Thou wilt not murder me? Help, help, ho!

POLONIUS: (*Within*) What ho! Help, help, help!

HAMLET: How now, a rat? (*Draws his sword*) Dead for a ducat, dead!
Makes a pass through the arras.

POLONIUS: (*Behind*) O, I am slain. (*Falls and dies.*)

QUEEN: O me, what hast thou done?

HAMLET: Nay, I know not: is it the King?

Lifts up the arras and draws forth Polonius.

QUEEN: O, what a rash and bloody deed is this.

HAMLET: A bloody deed! Almost as bad, good mother, as kill a king and marry his brother.

QUEEN: As kill a king?

HAMLET: Ay lady, 'twas my word. – Thou wretched, rash, intruding fool, farewell! I took thee for thy better: take thy fortune. Leave wringing of your hands: peace! Sit you down and let me wring your heart: for so I shall, if it be made of penetrable stuff.

QUEEN: What have I done, that thou dare'st wag thy tongue in noise so rude against me?

HAMLET: Such an act that blurs the grace and blush of modesty; calls virtue hypocrite; takes off the rose from the fair forehead of an innocent love and sets a blister there; makes marriage vows as false as dicers' oaths.

QUEEN: Ah me, what act, that roars so loud and thunders in the index?

HAMLET: Look here upon this picture, and on this, the counterfeit presentment of two brothers. See what a grace was seated on this brow – to give the world assurance of a man: this was your husband. Look you now what follows: here is your husband, like a mildewed ear blasting his wholesome brother. Have you eyes? Could you on this fair mountain leave to feed, and batten on this moor? Ha! Have you eyes? You cannot call it love, for at your age the heyday in the blood is tame, it's humble, and waits upon the judgement; and what judgement would step from this to this? What devil was't that thus hath cozened you at hoodman-blind?

QUEEN: O Hamlet, speak no more. Thou turn'st mine eyes into my very soul; and there I see such black and grained spots as will not leave their tinct.

HAMLET: Nay, but to live in the rank sweat of an enseamed bed, stewed in corruption, honeying and making love over the nasty sty –

QUEEN: O speak to me no more; these words, like daggers, enter in mine ears; no more, sweet Hamlet!

HAMLET: A murderer and a villain; a slave, that is not twentieth part the tithe of your precedent lord: a vice of kings; a cutpurse of the empire and the rule, that from a shelf the precious diadem stole, and put in his pocket!

QUEEN: No more!

HAMLET: A king of shreds and patches –

Enter Ghost.

Save me and hover o'er me with your wings, you heavenly guards! – What would you, gracious figure?

QUEEN: Alas, he's mad!

HAMLET: Do you not come your tardy son to chide that, lapsed in time and passion, lets go by the important acting of your dread command? O, say!

GHOST: Do not forget: this visitation is but to whet thy almost blunted purpose. But look, amazement on thy mother sits: speak to her, Hamlet.

HAMLET: How is it with you, lady?

QUEEN: Alas, how is't with you, that you do bend your eye on vacancy, and with the incorporal air do hold discourse? O gentle son, upon the heat and flame of thy distemper sprinkle cool patience. Whereon do you look?

HAMLET: On him, on him! Look you, how pale he glares!

QUEEN: To whom do you speak this?

HAMLET: Do you see nothing there?

QUEEN: Nothing at all; yet all that is I see.

HAMLET: Nor did you nothing hear?

QUEEN: No, nothing but ourselves.

HAMLET: Why, look you there! Look, how it steals away! My father in his
    habit as he lived! Look, where he goes even now out at the portal!

Exit Ghost.

QUEEN: This is the very coinage of your brain: this bodiless creation
    ecstasy is very cunning in.

HAMLET: Ecstasy! My pulse, as yours, doth temperately keep time, and
    makes as healthful music: Mother, for love of grace, lay not a
    flattering unction to your soul, that not your trespass but my
    madness speaks: it will but skin and film the ulcerous place,
    whilst rank corruption, mining all within, infects unseen.
    Confess yourself to heaven; repent what's past; avoid what is
    to come; and do not spread the compost on the weeds, to make
    them ranker.

QUEEN: O Hamlet, thou hast cleft my heart in twain.

HAMLET: O, throw away the worser part of it, and live the purer with
    the other half. Good night; but go not to mine uncle's bed:
    refrain tonight, and that shall lend a kind of easiness to the
    next abstinence, the next more easy. Once more, good night,
    and when you are desirous to be blessed, I'll blessing beg of you.
    – For this same lord, I do repent: but heaven hath pleased it so.
    I will bestow him, and will answer well the death I gave him.
    So again, good night. – One word more, good lady.

QUEEN: What shall I do?

HAMLET: Not this, by no means, that I bid you do: let the bloat King tempt you again to bed, pinch wanton on your cheek, call you his mouse, and let him, for a pair of reechy kisses, or paddling in your neck with his damned fingers, make you ravel all this matter out, that I essentially am not in madness, but mad in craft. – I must to England; you know that?

QUEEN: Alack, I had forgot, 'tis so concluded on.

HAMLET: There's letters sealed: and my two school-fellows (whom I will trust as I will adders fanged), they bear the mandate; they must sweep my way and marshal me to knavery: let it work. – I'll lug the guts into the neighbour room. Mother, good night. Indeed, this counsellor is now most still, most secret, and most grave, who was in life a foolish prating knave. Come, sir, to draw toward an end with you. Good night, mother.

Exeunt severally. Hamlet dragging out the body of Polonius.

SCENE 12 'THERE'S MATTER'

The King's Dressing Room.

KING: There's matter in these sighs, these profound heaves: you must translate: 'tis fit we understand them. Where is your son?

QUEEN: Ah, good my lord, what have I seen tonight!

KING: What, Gertrude? How does Hamlet?

QUEEN: Mad as the sea and wind when both contend which is the mightier. In this lawless fit, behind the arras hearing something stir, he whips his rapier out, and cries 'A rat, a rat!', and in his brainish apprehension kills the unseen good old man.

KING: O heavy deed! It had been so with us, had we been there. Alas, how shall this bloody deed be answered? It will be laid to us, whose providence should have kept short, restrained, and out of haunt this mad young man. Where is he gone?

QUEEN: To draw apart the body he hath killed: o'er whom his very madness, like some ore among a mineral of metals base, shows itself pure: he weeps for what is done.

KING: O Gertrude, come away! The sun no sooner shall the mountains touch but we will ship him hence: and this vile deed we must, with all our majesty and skill, both countenance and excuse. Ho, Guildenstern!

Enter Rosencrantz and Guildenstern.

Friends both, go join you with some further aid: Hamlet in madness hath Polonius slain, and from his mother's closet hath he dragged him. Go seek him out, speak fair, and bring the body into the chapel. I pray you, haste in this.

SCENE 13 'SAFELY STOWED'

The Council Chamber. Enter Hamlet.

HAMLET: Safely stowed.

ROSENCRANTZ AND GUILDENSTERN: (*Within*) Hamlet! Lord Hamlet!

HAMLET: What noise? Who calls on Hamlet? O, here they come.

Enter Rosencrantz and Guildenstern.

ROSENCRANTZ: What have you done, my lord, with the dead body?

HAMLET: Compounded it with dust, whereto 'tis kin.

ROSENCRANTZ: Tell us where 'tis, that we may take it thence, and bear it to the chapel.

HAMLET: Do not believe it.

ROSENCRANTZ: Believe what?

HAMLET: That I can keep your counsel and not mine own. Besides, to be demanded of a sponge – what replication should be made by the son of a king?

ROSENCRANTZ: Take you me for a sponge, my lord?

HAMLET: Ay, sir, that soaks up the King's countenance, his rewards, his authorities.

ROSENCRANTZ: My lord, you must tell us where the body is, and go with us to the King.

HAMLET: The body is with the King, but the King is not with the body. The King is a thing –

GUILDENSTERN: A thing, my lord?

HAMLET: Of nothing.

Enter King and Queen.

KING: Now, Hamlet, where's Polonius?

HAMLET: At supper!

KING: At supper! Where?

HAMLET: Not where he eats, but where he is eaten: a certain convocation of politic worms are at him.

KING: Where is Polonius?

HAMLET: In heaven: send thither to see: if your messenger find him not there, seek him in the other place yourself. But, indeed, if you find him not within this month, you shall nose him as you go up the stairs to the lobby.

KING: Go seek him there.

HAMLET: He will stay till you come.

Exit Guildenstern.

KING: Hamlet, this deed of thine, for thine especial safety (which we do tender, as we dearly grieve for that which thou hast done), must send thee hence with fiery quickness: therefore prepare thyself for England.

HAMLET: For England!

KING: Ay, Hamlet.

HAMLET: Good.

KING: So is it, if thou knew'st our purposes.

HAMLET: I see a cherub that sees them. But come; for England! Farewell, dear mother.

QUEEN: Thy loving father, Hamlet.

HAMLET: My mother: father and mother is man and wife; man and wife is one flesh; and so, my mother. Come, for England!

Exit Hamlet.

KING: Follow him at foot; tempt him with speed abroad; delay it not. I'll have him hence tonight: away! For everything is sealed and done that else leans on the affair: pray you, make haste.

Exit Rosencrantz.

And England, if my love thou hold'st at aught, thou may'st not coldly set our sovereign process, which imports at full, by letters conjuring to that effect, the present death of Hamlet. Do it, England; for like the hectic in my blood he rages, and thou must cure me: till I know 'tis done, howe'er my haps, my joys were ne'er begun.

SCENE 14 'NEW SCENE'[19]

*A plain in Denmark [including an army marching]. Enter Hamlet,
Rosencrantz, Guildenstern and others.*

HAMLET: Good sir, whose powers are these?

ROSENCRANTZ: They are of Norway, sir.

HAMLET: How purposed sir, I pray you?

GUILDENSTERN: Against some part of Poland.

HAMLET: Who commands them, sir?

ROSENCRANTZ: The nephew of old Norway, Fortinbras.

HAMLET: Goes it against the main of Poland, sir, or [for] some frontier?

ROSENCRANTZ: Truly to speak, sir, and with no addition, they[20] go to
gain a little patch of ground that hath in it no profit but the
name. To pay five ducats, five, I would not farm it, nor will
it yield to Norway or the Pole a ranker rate, should it be sold
in fee.

HAMLET: Why then, the Polack never will defend it.

ROSENCRANTZ: Yes, 'tis already garrisoned.

HAMLET: Two thousand souls and twenty thousand ducats will not
debate the question of this straw; this is th' imposthume of
much wealth and peace, that inward breaks, and shows no
cause without why the man dies. I humbly thank you, sir.

ROSENCRANTZ: God be wi' you, sir.

GUILDENSTERN: Will't please you go, my lord?

HAMLET: I'll be with you straight. Go a little before.

Exeunt all but Hamlet.

---

19   A late insertion for the 1943 revival production and used thereafter. In the original
play, Hamlet converses with a Norwegian captain, Guildenstern is silent and Rosencrantz only contributes the line 'Will'it please you go, my lord?'.

20   Originally 'we'.

HAMLET: How all occasions do inform against me and spur my dull
revenge! What is man, if his chief good and market of his time
be but to sleep and feed? A beast, no more. Sure, he that made
us with such large discourse, looking before and after, gave
us not that capability and godlike reason to fust in us unused.
Now, whether it be bestial oblivion, or some craven scruple
of thinking too precisely on th' event – a thought which,
quarter'd, hath but one part wisdom and ever three parts
coward – I do not know why yet I live to say 'This thing's to do';
sith I have cause, and will, and strength, and means to do't.
Examples gross as earth exhort me. Witness this army of such
mass and charge, led by a delicate and tender prince, whose
spirit, with divine ambition puff'd, makes mouths at the
invisible event; exposing what is mortal and unsure to all that
fortune, death, and danger dare, even for an eggshell. Rightly
to be great is not to stir without great argument, but greatly to
find quarrel in a straw when honour's at the stake. How stand
I, then, that have a father kill'd, a mother stain'd, excitements
of my reason and my blood, and let all sleep, while, to my
shame, I see the imminent death of twenty thousand men, that
for a fantasy and trick of fame go to their graves like beds?
O, from this time forth, my thoughts be bloody, or be nothing
worth!

SCENE 15 'MAD SCENE'

The Council Chamber. Enter Queen and Horatio.

QUEEN: I will not speak with her.

HORATIO: She is importunate, indeed distract: her mood will needs be pitied.

QUEEN: What would she have?

HORATIO: She speaks much of her father. 'Twere good she were spoken with, for she may strew dangerous conjectures in ill-breeding minds.[21]

QUEEN: Let her come in.

Exit Horatio.

To my sick soul, as sin's true nature is, each toy seems prologue to some great amiss: so full of artless jealousy is guilt, it spills itself in fearing to be spilt.

Re-enter Horatio with Ophelia.

OPHELIA: Where is the beauteous majesty of Denmark?

QUEEN: How now, Ophelia?

OPHELIA: Say you? Nay, pray you, mark.

(*Singing*)

How should I your true love know

From another one?

By his cockle hat and staff,

And his sandal shoon.

QUEEN: Alas, sweet lady, what imports this song?

OPHELIA: (*Singing*)

He is dead and gone, lady,

He is dead and gone;

---

21   Originally ''Twere good … minds' was spoken by Gertrude.

> At his head a grass-green turf,
>
> At his heels a stone.
>
> O,oh!

QUEEN: Nay, but Ophelia –

Enter King.

QUEEN: Alas, look here, my lord.

OPHELIA: (*Singing*)

> Larded with sweet flowers;
>
> Which bewept to the ground did [not] go
>
> With true-love showers.

KING: How do you, pretty lady?

OPHELIA: Well, God 'ild you! They say the owl was a baker's daughter.
Lord, we know what we are, but know not what we may be.
God be at your table!

KING: Conceit upon her father.

OPHELIA: I hope all will be well. We must be patient, but I cannot
choose but weep to think they should lay him in the cold ground.
My brother shall know of it; and so I thank you for your good
counsel. Come, my coach! Good night, ladies! Good night, sweet
ladies, good night, good night.

Exit Ophelia.

KING: Follow her close; give her good watch, I pray you.

Exit Horatio.

O this is the poison of deep grief; it springs all from her father's
death. O Gertrude, Gertrude, when sorrows come, they come
not single spies, but in battalions. First, her father slain; next,
your son gone, and he most violent author of his own just
remove; the people muddied, thick and unwholesome in their
thoughts and whispers for good Polonius' death; and we have

done but greenly in hugger-mugger to inter him; poor Ophelia divided from herself and her fair judgement; last, and as much containing as all these, her brother is in secret come from France. O my dear Gertrude, this, like to a murdering-piece, in many places gives me superfluous death.

A noise within.

QUEEN: Alack, what noise is this?

Enter Horatio.

KING: Where are thy Switzers? Let them guard the door. What is the matter?

HORATIO: Save yourself, my lord: the ocean, overpeering of his list, eats not the flats with more impetuous haste than young Laertes, in a riotous head, o'erbears your officers. The rabble call him lord, and cry 'Choose we! Laertes shall be king!' Caps, hands, and tongues applaud it to the clouds, 'Laertes shall be king! Laertes king!'

Noise within.

QUEEN: How cheerfully on the false trail they cry! O, this is counter, you false Danish dogs!

Enter Laertes, armed; Danes following.

LAERTES: Where is this king? – Sirs, stand you all without.

DANES: No, let's come in.

LAERTES: I pray you, give me leave.

DANES: We will, we will.

They retire without the door.

LAERTES: I thank you: keep the door. O thou vile king, give me my father!

QUEEN: *[Restraining Laertes]* Calmly, good Laertes.

KING: What is the cause, Laertes, that thy rebellion looks so giant-
　　like? Let him go, Gertrude. Tell me, Laertes, why thou art thus
　　incensed: – let him go, Gertrude: – speak, man.

LAERTES: Where is my father?

KING: Dead.

QUEEN: But not by him.

KING: Let him demand his fill.

LAERTES: How came he dead? I'll not be juggled with! To hell,
　　allegiance! Vows, to the blackest devil! Conscience and grace, to
　　the profoundest pit! I dare damnation. To this point I stand, that
　　both the worlds I give to negligence, let come what comes; only
　　I'll be revenged most thoroughly for my father.

KING: Who shall stay you?

LAERTES: My will, not all the world.

KING: Good Laertes, if you desire to know the certainty of your dear
　　father's death, is't writ in your revenge that, sweepstake, you
　　will draw both friend and foe, winner and loser?

LAERTES: None but his enemies.

KING: Why, now you speak like a good child and a true gentleman.
　　That I am guiltless of your father's death and am most sensibly
　　in grief for it, it shall as level to your judgement pierce, as day
　　does your eye.

COURTIER: *[Within]* Let her come in.

　　Re-enter Ophelia.

LAERTES: Dear maid; kind sister; sweet Ophelia!

OPHELIA: (*Singing*)

　　They bore him barefaced on the bier,
　　Hey non nony, nony, hey nony,

> And on his grave rained many a tear –
> Fare you well, my dove.

LAERTES: Hadst thou thy wits, and didst persuade revenge, it could not move thus.

OPHELIA: You must sing 'A-down, a-down', and you call him a-down-a'.
> – There's rosemary, that's for remembrance. Pray, love, remember: and there is pansies, that's for thoughts.

LAERTES: A document in madness.

OPHELIA: There's fennel for you, and columbines: there's rue for you, and here's some for me: we may call it herb of grace o' Sundays.
> – O, you must wear your rue with a difference. – There's a daisy: I would give you some violets, but they withered all when my father died: they say he made a good end. (*Singing*)
> For bonny sweet Robin is all my joy.

LAERTES: Thought and affliction, passion, hell itself, she turns to favour and to prettiness.

OPHELIA: (*Singing*)
> And will he not come back again?
> And will he not come back again?
> No, no, he is dead;
> Go to thy death-bed;
> He will never come again.
>
> His beard was as white as snow,
> All flaxen was his poll:
> He is gone, he is gone,
> And we cast away moan:
> God ha' mercy on his soul!

And of all Christian souls! I pray God – Go be wi' ye.[22]

Exit Ophelia.

LAERTES: Do you see this, O God?

KING: Laertes, I must commune with your grief, or you deny me right. Go but apart, make choice of whom your wisest friends you will, and they shall hear and judge 'twixt you and me.

LAERTES: Let this be so: his means of death, his obscure funeral, cry to be heard, as 'twere from heaven to earth, that I must call't in question.

KING: So you shall: and where the offence is, let the great axe fall. I pray you, go with me.

SCENE 16 'PLOTTING'

A room in the castle. Enter King and Laertes.

[KING: Now must your conscience my acquittal seal, and you must put me in your heart for friend, sith you have heard, and with a knowing ear, that he which hath your noble father slain pursued my life.] [23]

LAERTES: It well appears – but tell me why you proceeded not against these feats, so crimeful and so capital in nature.

KING: O, for two special reasons, which may to you, perhaps, seem much unsinewed, but yet to me they are strong. The Queen his mother, lives almost by his looks. The other motive, why to a public count I might not go, is the great love the general gender bear him.

LAERTES: And so I have a noble father lost, a sister driven into desperate terms. But my revenge will come.

---

22 Originally 'God buy you'.
23 Omitted in Marsh's typescript.

KING: Break not your sleep[24] for that.

> *Enter a Messenger.*

> How now! What news?

MESSENGER: Letters, my lord, from Hamlet: this to your majesty, this to the Queen.

KING: From Hamlet! Who brought them?

MESSENGER: Sailors, my lord, they say.

KING: Laertes, you shall hear them. Leave us.

> *Exit Messenger. [He reads]*

> 'High and mighty, you shall know I am set naked on your kingdom. Tomorrow shall I beg leave to see your kingly eyes: when I shall, first asking your pardon thereunto, recount the occasions of my sudden and more strange return.
>
> Hamlet.'
>
> What should this mean? Are all the rest come back? Or is it some abuse, and no such thing?

LAERTES: Know you the hand?

KING: 'Tis Hamlet's character – 'Naked' – and in a postscript here he says: 'Alone'. Can you advise me?

LAERTES: I'm lost in it, my lord. But let him come; it warms the very sickness in my heart, that I shall live and tell him to his teeth, 'Thus didest thou'.

KING: If it be so, Laertes, will you be ruled by me?

LAERTES: Ay, my lord, so you will not o'errule me to a peace.

KING: To thine own peace. I will work him to an exploit, now ripe in my device, under the which he shall not choose but fall: and for his death no wind of blame shall breathe, but even his mother shall uncharge the practice and call it accident.

---

24 Originally 'sleeps'.

LAERTES: My lord, I will be ruled; the rather, if you could devise it so, that I might be the organ.

KING: It falls right. You have been talked of since your travel much, and that in Hamlet's hearing, for a quality wherein they say, you shine.

LAERTES: What part is that, my lord?

KING: Two months since here was a gentleman of Normandy –

LAERTES: A Norman was't? – Upon my life, Lamond.[25]

KING: The very same.

LAERTES: I know him well.

KING: He made confession of you, and gave you such a masterly report for art and exercise in your defence, and for your rapier most especially, that he cried out 'twould be a sight indeed if one could match you. This report of his did Hamlet so envenom with his envy, that he could nothing do but wish and beg your sudden coming o'er to play with him. Now, out of this –

LAERTES: What out of this, my lord?

KING: Hamlet comes back. What would you undertake, to show yourself your father's son in deed more than in words?

LAERTES: To cut his throat i' the church.

KING: No place indeed should murder sanctuarize; revenge should have no bounds. But, good Laertes, will you do this? Keep close within your chamber. Hamlet, returned, shall know you are come home. We'll put on those shall praise your excellence, and wager on your heads: he, being remiss, most generous, and free from all contriving, will not peruse the foils; so that with ease, or with a little shuffling, you may choose a sword unbated, and, in pass of practice, requite him for your father.

---

25 Originally variously 'Lamord' or 'Lamound', 'Lamond' in Irving.

LAERTES: I will do't; and, for that purpose, I'll anoint my sword.
I bought an unction of a mountebank, so mortal, that but a dip of knife in it, where it draws blood no cataplasm so rare can save the thing from death that is but scratched withal: I'll touch my point with this contagion, that, if I gall him slightly, it may be death.

KING: Let's further think of this. If this should fail, 'twere better not assayed: therefore this project should have a back or second, that might hold, if this should blast in proof. Soft! Let me see. We'll make a solemn wager on your cunnings – I ha't. When in your motion you are hot and dry (as make your bouts more violent to that end) and that he calls for drink, I'll have prepared for him[26] a chalice for the nonce; whereon but sipping, if he by chance escape your venomed stuck, our purpose may hold there.
Enter Queen.
How now, sweet Queen?

QUEEN: One woe doth tread upon another's heel, so fast they follow: your sister's drowned, Laertes.

LAERTES: Drowned!

QUEEN: There is a willow grows aslant a brook, that shows his hoar leaves in the glassy stream; there, with fantastic garlands did she come: there, on the pendent boughs her coronet weeds clambering to hang, an envious sliver broke; when down her weedy trophies and herself fell in the weeping brook. Her clothes spread wide; and, mermaid-like, awhile they bore her up; which time she chanted snatches of old tunes: but long it could not be till that her garments, heavy with their drink, pulled the poor wretch from her melodious lay to muddy death.

---

26   Originally 'prepared him'.

LAERTES: Alas, then, she is drowned?

QUEEN: Drowned, drowned.

LAERTES: Too much of water hast thou, poor Ophelia, and therefore
I forbid my tears: but yet it is our trick; nature her custom holds,
let shame say what it will. *[He weeps]* When these are gone, the
woman will be out. Adieu, my lord.

Exit Laertes.

KING: Let's follow, Gertrude: how much I had to do to calm his rage!
Now fear I this will give him start again; therefore let's follow.

SCENE 17 'GRAVEYARD'

A graveyard. Enter two Clowns, gravediggers.

FIRST CLOWN: Is she to be buried in Christian burial that wilfully seeks
her own salvation?

SECOND CLOWN: I tell thee she is: and therefore make her grave straight:
the crowner hath sat on her, and finds it Christian burial.

FIRST CLOWN: How can that be, unless she drowned herself in her
own defence?

SECOND CLOWN: Why 'tis found so.

FIRST CLOWN: It must be *so offendendo*, it cannot be else. For here lies
the point: if I drown myself wittingly, it argues an act; and
an act hath three branches; it is to act, to do, and to perform:
therefore,[27] she drowned herself wittingly.

SECOND CLOWN: Nay, but hear you, Goodman Delver –[28]

FIRST CLOWN: Give me leave. Here lies the water – good: here stands the
man – good: If the man go to this water and drown himself, it is,

---

27 Originally 'argal', the clown's form of 'ergo'; again at 'therefore, he that is not guilty'
below.
28 Marsh has 'but here you, good man, delver'.

will he nill he, he goes – mark you that: but if the water come to him and drown him, he drowns not himself: therefore, he that is not guilty of his own death shortens not his own life.

SECOND CLOWN: What, is this the law?[29]

FIRST CLOWN: Ay, marry it is; crowner's quest law – come, my spade. Go, get thee to Yaughan;[30] fetch me a stoup of liquor.

Exit Second Clown. Enter Hamlet and Horatio.

FIRST CLOWN: (*Singing*)

In youth when I did love, did love,

Methought it was very sweet,

To contract, O, the time for, ah, my behove,

O, methought there was nothing meet.

HAMLET: Has this fellow no feeling for his business that he sings at grave-making?

HORATIO: Custom hath made it in him a property of easiness.

HAMLET: 'Tis e'en so: the hand of little employment hath the daintier sense.

FIRST CLOWN: (*Singing*)

But age, with his stealing steps,

Hath clawed me in his clutch,

And hath shipped me intil the land,

As if I had never been such.

Throws up a skull.

HAMLET: That skull had a tongue in it, and could sing once. It might be the pate of a politician, which this ass now o'er-reaches: one that would circumvent God, might it not?

HORATIO: It might, my lord.

---

29 Originally 'But is this law?'.
30 Possibly the name of a local publican.

HAMLET: Or of a courtier, which could say, 'Good morrow, sweet lord! How dost thou, good lord?'

HORATIO: Ay, my lord.

HAMLET: Why, e'en so: and now my Lady Worm's, chapless, and knocked about the mazard with a sexton's spade – I will speak to this fellow. Whose grave is this?

FIRST CLOWN: Mine, sir. (*Sings*)

O, a pit of clay for to be made

For such a guest is meet.

HAMLET: I think it be thine indeed, for thou liest in it.

FIRST CLOWN: You lie out on't, sir, and therefore it is not yours: for my part, I do not lie in it, and yet it is mine.

HAMLET: 'Tis for the dead, not for the quick; therefore thou liest.

FIRST CLOWN: 'Tis a quick lie, sir, 'twill away again from me to you.

HAMLET: What man dost thou dig it for?

FIRST CLOWN: No man, sir.

HAMLET: What woman, then?

FIRST CLOWN: For none, neither.

HAMLET: Who is to be buried in it?

FIRST CLOWN: One that was a woman, sir; but, rest her soul, she's dead.

HAMLET: How absolute the knave is! – How long hast thou been a grave-maker?

FIRST CLOWN: Of all the days in the year, I came to it that day that our last king Hamlet o'ercame Fortinbras.

HAMLET: How long is that since?

FIRST CLOWN: Cannot you tell that? Every fool can tell that: it was the very day that young Hamlet was born; he that is mad and sent into England.

HAMLET: Ay, marry. Why was he sent into England?

FIRST CLOWN: Why because he was mad: he shall recover his wits there, or if he do not, it's no great matter there.

HAMLET: Why?

FIRST CLOWN: 'Twill not be seen in him there: there the men are as mad as he.

HAMLET: How came he mad?

FIRST CLOWN: Very strangely, they say.

HAMLET: How strangely?

FIRST CLOWN: 'Faith, e'en with losing his wits.

HAMLET: Upon what ground?

FIRST CLOWN: Why, here in Denmark: I have been sexton here, man and boy, thirty years.

HAMLET: How long will a man lie in the earth ere he rot?

FIRST CLOWN: 'Faith, if he be not rotten before he die, he will last you some eight or nine year[31] – Here's a skull now: this skull has lain in the earth three and twenty years.

HAMLET: Whose was it?

FIRST CLOWN: A mad[32] fellow's it was: whose do you think it was?

HAMLET: Nay, I know not.

FIRST CLOWN: A pestilence on him for a mad rogue! He poured a flagon of Rhenish on my head once. This same skull, sir, was Yorick's skull, the King's jester.

HAMLET: This?

FIRST CLOWN: E'en that.

HAMLET: Let me see. (*Takes up the skull*) Alas, poor Yorick! I knew him, Horatio: a fellow of infinite jest, of most excellent fancy: he hath borne me on his back a thousand times: and now how abhorred in my imagination it is! My gorge rises at it. Here hung those

---

31 Originally 'some eight year or nine year'.
32 Originally 'whoreson mad'.

lips, that I have kissed I know not how oft. Where are your jibes now, your gambols, your songs, your flashes of merriment that were wont to set the table on a roar? Not one now to mock your own grinning? Quite chop-fallen? Now get you to my lady's chamber and tell her, let her paint an inch thick, to this favour she must come. Make her laugh at that. Prithee, Horatio, tell me one thing.

HORATIO: What's that, my lord?

HAMLET: Dost thou think Alexander looked o' this fashion in the earth?

HORATIO: E'en so.

HAMLET: And smelt so? Pah!

He puts the skull down.

HORATIO: E'en so, my lord.

HAMLET: To what base uses we may return, Horatio.

 Imperial Caesar, dead and turned to clay,

 Might stop a hole to keep the wind away.

 O, that that earth, which kept the world in awe,

 Should patch a wall t'expel the winter's flaw.[33]

 But soft, but soft: aside: here comes the King.

Enter Priest etc. in procession: the corpse of Ophelia: Laertes and Mourners following: King, Queen and their trains.

HAMLET: The Queen, the courtiers. Who is that they follow? And with such maimed rites? This doth betoken the corpse they follow did with desperate hand fordo its own life: 'twas of some estate. Couch we awhile, and mark.

Retires with Horatio.

LAERTES: What ceremony else?

HAMLET: That is Laertes, a very noble youth: mark.

---

33 The verse is a later insertion by Marsh.

LAERTES: What ceremony else?

PRIEST: No more be done: we should profane the service of the dead, to sing sage requiem, and such rest to her as to peace-parted souls.

LAERTES: Lay her i' the earth, and from her fair and unpolluted flesh may violets spring! I tell thee, churlish priest, a ministering angel shall my sister be, when thou liest howling.

HAMLET: What, the fair Ophelia!

QUEEN: Sweets to the sweet: farewell! (*Scattering flowers*) I hoped thou shouldst have been my Hamlet's wife: I thought thy bride-bed to have decked, sweet maid, and not have strewed thy grave.

LAERTES: O, treble woe fall ten times treble on that cursed head, whose wicked dead thy most ingenious sense deprived thee of! Hold off the earth awhile – (*leaping into the grave*)

HAMLET: (*Advancing*) What is he, whose grief bears such an emphasis, whose phrase of sorrow conjures the wandering stars and makes them stand, like wonder-wounded hearers? This is I, Hamlet the Dane.[34]

LAERTES: (*Leaping out of the grave and grappling with him*) The devil take thy soul!

HAMLET: Thou pray'st not well. I prithee take thy fingers from my throat; for though I am not splenative and rash, yet have I something in me dangerous, which let thy wisdom fear: hold off thy hand.

KING: Pluck them asunder.

QUEEN: Hamlet, Hamlet!

ALL: Gentlemen –

HORATIO: Good my lord, be quiet.

---

34 Sentence heavily underlined in Marsh.

The Attendants part them.[35]

HAMLET: Why, I will fight with him upon this theme, until my eyelids
will no longer wag.

QUEEN: O, my son, what theme?

HAMLET: I loved Ophelia, forty thousand brothers could not with their
quality of love make up my sum. What wilt thou do for her?

KING: O, he is mad, Laertes.

QUEEN: For love of God, forbear him.

HAMLET: 'Swounds, show we what thou'lt do. Dost thou come here to
whine? To outface me? Be buried quick with her and so will I.
Nay, and thou'lt mouth, I'll rant as well as thou.[36]

QUEEN: This is mere madness: and thus a while the fit will work on
him; anon, as patient as a female dove, when that her golden
couplets are disclosed, his silence will sit drooping.

HAMLET: Hear you, sir: what is the reason that you use me thus? I loved
you ever; but it is no matter: let Hercules himself do what he
may, the cat will mew, and the dog will have his day.

Exit Hamlet.

KING: I pray you, good Horatio, wait upon him.

Exit Horatio.

(*To Laertes*) Strengthen your patience in our last night's speech;
we'll put the matter to the present push. – Good Gertrude,
set some watch over your son. This grave shall have a living
monument. An hour of quiet shortly shall we see; till then in
patience our proceeding be.

---

35 This stage direction originally reads 'The Attendants part them and they come out of
the grave' but the previous stage direction has Laertes leap from the grave to attack
Hamlet.

36 Marsh has 'and so will I, so, and thou'lt mouth'.

SCENE 18 'DUEL'

A hall in the castle. Enter Hamlet and Horatio.

HAMLET: So much for this, sir; now shall you see the other. You do remember all the circumstance?

HORATIO: Remember it, my lord?

HAMLET: Sir, in my heart there was a kind of fighting that would not let me sleep. Rashly, and praised be rashness for it; let us know our indiscretion sometimes serves us well, when our dear plots do pall; and that should teach us there's a divinity that shapes our ends, rough-hew them how we will.

HORATIO: That is most certain.

HAMLET: Up from my cabin, my sea-gown scarfed about me, in the dark groped I to find out them, had my desire, fingered their packet, and, in fine, withdrew to mine own room again, making so bold, my fears forgetting manners, to unseal their grand commission; where I found, Horatio – O, royal knavery! – an exact command, larded with many several sorts of reason, importing Denmark's health and England's too, that, on the supervise, no leisure bated, I there should be dispatched.[37]

HORATIO: Is't possible? Why, what a king is this!

HAMLET: Does it not, think'st thee, stand me now upon – he that hath killed my king, and wronged[38] my mother; popped in between the election of my hopes; thrown out his angle for my proper life, and with such cozenage – is't not perfect conscience, to quit him with this arm?

HORATIO: It must be shortly known to him from England what is the issue of the business there.

---

37 Originally 'My head should be struck off'.
38 Originally 'whored'.

HAMLET: It will be short: the interim is mine; and a man's life no more than to say 'one'. But I am very sorry, good Horatio, that to Laertes I forgot myself; for, by the image of my cause, I see the portraiture of thine:[39] I'll count his favours: but sure the bravery of his grief did put me into a towering passion.

HORATIO: Who comes here?

Enter Osric.

OSRIC: Your lordship is right welcome back to Denmark.

HAMLET: I humbly thank you, sir. – Dost know this waterfly?

HORATIO: No, my good lord.

HAMLET: Thy state is the more gracious, for 'tis a vice to know him.

OSRIC: Sweet lord, if your lordship were at leisure, I should impart a thing to you from his majesty.

HAMLET: I will receive it, sir, with all diligence of spirit.

OSRIC: Sir, here is newly come to court Laertes; believe me, an absolute gentleman, for you shall find in him the continent of what part a gentleman would see.

HAMLET: Sir, his definement suffers no perdition in you: though, I know, to divide him inventorially would dizzy the arithmetic of memory.

OSRIC: Your lordship speaks most infallibly of him.

HAMLET: The concernancy, sir? Why do we wrap the gentleman in our rawer breath?

OSRIC: Sir?

HORATIO: Is't not possible to understand in another tongue? You will do't sir, really.

HAMLET: What imports the nomination of this gentleman?

OSRIC: Of Laertes?

---

39 Originally 'his'.

HORATIO: His purse is empty already: all his golden words are spent.

HAMLET: Of him, sir.

OSRIC: You are not ignorant of what excellence Laertes is – I mean, sir, with his weapon; but in his imputation laid on him by them, in his need he's unfellowed.

HAMLET: What's his weapon?

OSRIC: Rapier or dagger.

HAMLET: That's two of his weapons: but, well.

OSRIC: The king, sir, hath wagered with him six Barbary horses: against the which he has imponed, as I take it, six French rapiers and poniards.

HAMLET: Six Barbary horses against six French swords; that's the French bet against the Danish. Why is this 'imponed',[40] as you call it?

OSRIC: The King, sir, hath laid that in a dozen passes between yourself and him, he shall not exceed you three hits: he hath laid on twelve for nine; and it would come to immediate trial, if your lordship would vouchsafe the answer.

HAMLET: How if I answer 'No'?

OSRIC: I mean, my lord, the opposition of your person in trial.

HAMLET: Sir, I will walk in the hall: if it please his majesty, it is the breathing time of day with me; let the foils be brought. The gentleman willing, and the king hold his purpose, I will win for him if I can; if not, I will gain nothing but my shame and the odd hits.

OSRIC: Shall I re-deliver you e'en so?

HAMLET: To this effect, sir, after what flourish your nature will.

OSRIC: I commend my duty to your lordship.

---

40   Means 'staked' or 'wagered', not 'pawned' as some editions imply.

HAMLET: Yours, yours.

> *Exit Osric.*

>> He does well to commend it himself; there are no tongues else
>> for his turn.

> *Enter a Lord.*

LORD: My lord, his majesty sends to know if your pleasure hold to play
with Laertes, or that you will take a longer time.

HAMLET: I am constant to my purposes: they follow the king's pleasure:
if his fitness speaks, mine is ready: now, or whensoever,
provided I be so able as now.

LORD: The king and queen and all are coming down.

HAMLET: In happy time.

LORD: The queen desires you to use some gentle entertainment to
Laertes, before you fall to play.

HAMLET: She well instructs me.

> *Exit Lord.*

HORATIO: You will lose this wager, my lord.

HAMLET: I do not think so; since he went to France, I have been in
continual practice; I shall win the odds. But thou wouldst not
think, how ill all's here about my heart: but it is no matter.

HORATIO: Nay, good my lord –

HAMLET: It is but foolery; but it is such a kind of gain-giving as would
perhaps trouble a woman.

HORATIO: If your mind dislike anything, obey it: I will forestall their
repair thither, and say you are not fit.

HAMLET: Not a whit: we defy augury: there is special providence in
the fall of a sparrow. If it be now, 'tis not to come; if it be not
to come, it will be now; if it be not now, yet it will come: the

readiness is all: since no man has aught of what he leaves, what is't to leave betimes? Let be.

Enter King, Queen, Laertes, Lords, and Osric with foils.

KING: Come, Hamlet, come, and take this hand from me.

The King puts the hand of Laertes into that of Hamlet.

HAMLET: Give me your pardon, sir: I have done you wrong; but pardon't as you are a gentleman. This presence knows, and you must needs have heard, how I am punished with sore distraction. What I have done, that might your nature, honour, and exception roughly wake,[41] I here proclaim was madness. Was't Hamlet wronged Laertes? Never Hamlet. Who does it, then? His madness: If't be so, Hamlet is of the faction that is wronged; his madness is poor Hamlet's enemy. Sir, in this audience, let my disclaiming from a purposed evil free me so far in your most generous thoughts, that I have shot mine arrow o'er the house, and hurt my brother.

LAERTES: I am satisfied in nature whose motive, in this case, should stir me most to my revenge: but in my terms of honour, I stand aloof; and will no reconcilement, till by some elder masters of known honour, I have a voice and precedent of peace to keep my name ungored. But till that time, I do receive your offered love like love, and will not wrong it.

HAMLET: I embrace it freely, and will this brother's wager frankly play. Give us the foils. Come on.

LAERTES: Come, one for me.

HAMLET: I'll be your foil, Laertes, in mine ignorance.

LAERTES: You mock me, sir.

HAMLET: No, by this hand.

---

41   Originally 'awake'.

KING: Give them the foils, young Osric. Cousin Hamlet, you know
the wager?

HAMLET: Very well, my lord; your grace has laid the odds o' the
weaker side.

KING: I do not fear it, I have seen you both: but since he is bettered,
we have therefore odds.

LAERTES: This is too heavy, let me see another.

HAMLET: This likes me well. These foils have all a length?

OSRIC: Ay, my good lord.

(*They prepare to play.*)

KING: Set me the stoups of wine upon that table: and you, the judges,
bear a wary eye.

HAMLET: Come on, sir.

LAERTES: Come, my lord.

(*They play.*)

HAMLET: One.

LAERTES: No.

HAMLET: Judgement.

OSRIC: A hit, a very palpable hit.

LAERTES: Well – again.

KING: Stay: give me drink – Hamlet, this pearl is thine; here's to thy
health. Give him the cup.

HAMLET: I'll play this bout first; set it by awhile. Come.

(*They play.*)

Another hit: what say you?

LAERTES: A touch, a touch, I do confess.

KING: Our son will win.

QUEEN: He's faint,[42] and scant of breath. Here, Hamlet, take my napkin,
    rub thy brows: the queen carouses to thy fortune, Hamlet.

HAMLET: Good madam!

KING: Gertrude, do not drink.

QUEEN: I will, my lord: I pray you pardon me.

    (*She drinks and offers the cup to Hamlet*)

KING: (*Aside*) It is the poisoned cup; it is too late.

HAMLET: I dare not drink yet, madam; by and by.

QUEEN: Come, let me wipe your face.

LAERTES: My lord, I'll hit him now.

KING: I do not think it.

LAERTES: (*Aside*) And yet it is almost against my conscience.

HAMLET: Come for the third, Laertes: but you dally: I pray you, pass
    with your best violence: I am afeared you make a wanton of me.

LAERTES: Say you so? Come on.

    (*They play.*)

OSRIC: Nothing, neither way.

LAERTES: Have at you now!

    Laertes wounds Hamlet; then, in scuffling, they change rapiers,
    and Hamlet wounds Laertes.

KING: Part them; they are incensed.

HAMLET: Nay, come again.

    The Queen rises, falls back.

OSRIC: Look to the Queen there.

HORATIO: They bleed on both sides. How is it, my lord?

OSRIC: How is it, Laertes?

LAERTES: Why, as a woodcock to mine own springe, Osric; I am justly
    killed with mine own treachery.

---

42 Originally 'fat'.

HAMLET: How does the Queen?

KING: She swoons to see thee bleed.

QUEEN: No, no, the drink, the drink! – O my dear Hamlet – the drink, the drink! – I am poisoned.

(Dies.)

HAMLET: O villainy! Treachery! Seek it out!

LAERTES: It is here, Hamlet: Hamlet, thou art slain: no medicine in the world can do thee good: in thee there is not half an hour of life: the treacherous instrument is in thy hand, unbated and envenomed: the foul practice hath turned itself on me: lo, here I lie, never to rise again: thy mother's poisoned: I can no more – the King, the King's to blame.

HAMLET: The point envenomed too! Then venom, do thy work.

Stabs the King.

ALL: Treason, treason!

KING: O yet defend me, friends: I am but hurt.

HAMLET: Here, thou incestuous, murderous, damned Dane, drink off this potion: is thy union here? Follow my mother.

King dies.

LAERTES: He is justly served: it is a poison tempered by himself. Exchange forgiveness with me, noble Hamlet: mine and my father's death come not upon thee, nor thine on me!

Dies.

HAMLET: Heaven make me free of it! I follow thee. I am dead, Horatio. Wretched Queen, adieu! You that look pale and tremble at this chance, that are but mutes or audience to this act, had I but time (as this fell sergeant, Death, is strict in his arrest), O, I could tell you – but let it be. Horatio, I am dead: thou livest; report me in my cause aright to the unsatisfied.

HORATIO: Never believe it: I am more an antique Roman than a Dane: here's yet some liquor left.

HAMLET: As thou'rt a man, give me the cup: let go: by heaven, I'll have it – O good Horatio, what a wounded name, things standing thus unknown, shall live behind me! If thou didst ever hold me in thy heart, absent thee from felicity awhile, and in this harsh world, draw thy breath in pain to tell my story – O, I die, Horatio: the potent poison quite o'er-crows my spirit – the rest is silence.

Dies.

HORATIO: Now cracks a noble heart. Good night, sweet prince, and flights of angels sing thee to thy rest! Let four captains bear Hamlet, like a soldier, to the stage; for he was likely, had he been put on, to have proved most royally and, for his passage, the soldiers' music, and the rites of war, speak loudly for him.

THE CANTERBURY UNIVERSITY COLLEGE
DRAMA SOCIETY

HAMLET

IN MODERN DRESS

LITTLE THEATRE

AUGUST 2nd, 3rd, 4th, 5th, 6th and 7th
1943

Left: 1. The programme for the opening season. *ATL, PA1-q-173-programme*

Bottom: 2. The stage design for the production. *ATL, fMS-154-1-cyclorama*

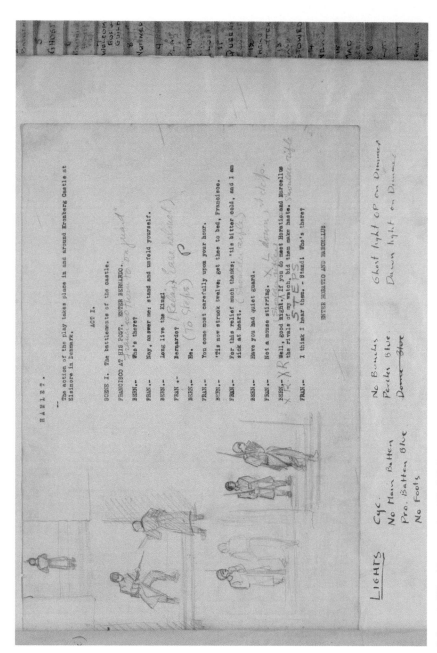

3. Page 1 of Marsh's typescript. ATL, fMS-154-1-1

Top: 4. Scene 1. Bernardo tells of seeing the ghost. *ATL, fMS-154-1-1-verso*

Bottom: 5. Scene 2. Cast photo: Hamlet is set apart because of the inward journey he is making. *ATL, PA1-q-173-3-1*

6. Scene 4. Hamlet determinedly follows his father's ghost. *Painting by Richard Lovell-Smith, courtesy of Richard Lovell-Smith Estate*

Top: 7. Scene 5. Hamlet, Horatio and Marcellus swear an oath of allegiance. *ATL, PA1-q-173-7-2*

Bottom: 8. Scene 9. Hamlet lays his head on Ophelia's lap. *ATL, fMS-154-4-36-verso*

9. Scene 9. The play within the play. *ATL, PA1-q-173-15*

10. Scene 17. Hamlet delivers the 'Alas, poor Yorick' speech. *ATL, PA1-q-173-21-1*

Top: 11. Scene 18. The duel that ends the play. *ATL, PA1-q-173-2*
Bottom: 12. Scene 18. Soldiers march off bearing Hamlet's body. *ATL, PA1-q-173-25*

DOUGLAS LILBURN'S INCIDENTAL MUSIC

Robert Hoskins

It was reported that Douglas Lilburn (1915–2001), who did more to create the voice of New Zealand art music than any other composer in the twentieth century, produced the incidental music to *Hamlet* within a few days of attending a single rehearsal.[1] Ngaio Marsh, however, spoke of his regular presence in the theatre before he set pen to paper:

> It took a bit of nerve for us to ask Douglas Lilburn if he would write the music for us but we did ask him and he agreed. He came and watched many rehearsals and then he stayed away and then he wrote, and what he wrote seemed to me really to be perfection. And, so it fell out, that one evening the cast came down to the theatre and they heard the sound of fiddles. The players were rehearsing and they were making sounds that seemed to us to be the very breath of the cold night air at Elsinore.[2]

Crisp nights were a commonplace for Lilburn, who grew up on Drysdale, a hill-country farm bordering the mountainous region of the central North Island, and who, as an undergraduate at Canterbury College, hiked down the West Coast in late autumn to reach the glaciers. The wartime atmosphere of Ngaio Marsh's production would also have resonated with the composer. As a student under Ralph

Vaughan Williams at the Royal College of Music, he had experienced the tensions of living in London when war was declared. Lilburn was rejected for military service because of poor eyesight; his brother, Euan, an RAF pilot, was killed in an air accident in 1940. That year, Lilburn composed his early major orchestral work, *Overture: Aotearoa*, which has become a New Zealand classic.

When he returned to Christchurch in 1942, Lilburn found himself in the arts centre of New Zealand. Here, in the company of poets, painters, publishers and theatre directors, he was determined to be a freelance composer, and he remained in the city for six years before moving to Wellington to join the staff of Victoria University College. He created works to which wartime and later audiences responded: *Landfall in Unknown Seas*, incidental music to a poem by Allen Curnow; *Elegy*, a song cycle on man's place in nature; and the First Symphony, opening with a clarion call, a declaration of independence addressed to all New Zealanders.

Marsh's typescript for *Hamlet* is rich in musical cues but, from the evidence of the completed score, Lilburn favoured less music in order to create maximum impact. Orchestrated for three violins and tubular bell, the score included five numbers: a mysterious nocturnal prologue (the bell strikes midnight) to the opening scene; a fanfare; two versions of a courtly march somewhat like the metrically rigid fourth movement in Vaughan Williams's *Flos Campi*; music for the play within the play, in which the melodic beauty gains in sonority through an accompaniment restricted to lute-like strums; and slow-step funereal music at the end to commemorate Hamlet as a fallen hero. The opening and closing music, and the players' music, are fixed, whereas the fanfare and march recur as required. In this way both the beginning, middle and end of the play, and the stage movement within scenes, are highlighted musically.[3] The violinists were Margaret Cicely, Nancy Browne and Eve Christeller, students of Maurice Claire, a friend of Lilburn who encouraged the composer to explore string technique; Lilburn played the bell.[4] The music was performed live for the Christchurch production but recorded for the later national tour; these recordings have not been traced.

Marsh never forgot her 'first delighted shock on hearing the magic he [Lilburn] called up for the battlements at Elsinore: how the sound flowed into the play and was an articulated element of the dialogue'.[5] Allen Curnow, reviewing the production for the *Listener*, was no less impressed.

> Lilburn's music for three violins, heard first as an overture, then between scenes and in a little sombre march for the entrance and exit of the Court, was very pure and clean sound, almost cold. It had the effect, even before the curtains parted, of making the mind clear for the tragedy to pass … It displayed the humility which is the proof, at times, of all real creativeness, seeming to gain power by submissive entrance into its great context.[6]

Lilburn subsequently composed music for all Ngaio Marsh's Shakespeare productions at Canterbury College through to 1946: *Othello*, *A Midsummer Night's Dream*, *Henry V* and *Macbeth*.[7] He later described it as 'a marvellous experience … you always learnt a tremendous amount about pace and form'.[8] Marsh, in hindsight, summed up Lilburn's contribution: 'Writing music for Shakespeare is a delicate undertaking. Far too often, even in otherwise distinguished productions, music is something tacked on, insisting, all too obviously, on mood or on its own self-importance or merely filling in a scenic change. Douglas's sound was an organic part of the play and exquisitely adjusted to it. Without his music the productions would have been bereft indeed.'[9]

Lilburn remembered that 'the good Ngaio always made me feel that whatever you did was the best thing possible'.[10] As he told a friend,

> She had more understanding of Shakespeare than anyone else I ever met, and an exquisite ear for the music and cadences of his verse (all other producers later experienced here or in London were proletarian by contrast). She was the most proficient producer I ever worked with, the most imaginative, most reliable, most generous, most loveable, and with some loving insight able to draw out of everyone she worked with the utmost they could give.[11]

Lilburn and Marsh remained friends. As David Sell recalled, when Lilburn revisited Christchurch to deliver an address at the inaugural meeting of the Christchurch Society for Contemporary Music, in the Great Hall of the University of Canterbury on 20 April 1967, he was taken to the Ilam campus to see the newly built Ngaio Marsh Theatre. Marsh, who happened to be there, called from the stage in her stentorian voice, 'Oh, Douglas!', then rushed to embrace him. Sell never forgot the spontaneity of their greeting.[12]

Lilburn made various arrangements of the dream-like players' music, in versions for piano, violin and viola, recorder, and string orchestra (the latter to popular effect as the first of Four Canzonas, *arranged 1980) but the* Hamlet *score has not previously been published. The copy-text for this edition is Lilburn's pencil holograph deposited in the Alexander Turnbull Library under the call number fMS-2483-032. Obvious slips and inconsistencies have been silently corrected. Editorial titles, tempo indications and dynamic markings are shown in square brackets.*

NOTES

1   *New Zealand Free Lance*, 24 November 1943, quoted in Valerie Harris and Philip Norman (eds), *Douglas Lilburn: A Festschrift for Douglas Lilburn on his retirement from the Victoria University of Wellington, January 31, 1980*, 2nd edn (Wellington: Composers' Association of New Zealand, 1980), p. 33.

2   Ngaio Marsh recalls her 'affectionate debt' to Douglas Lilburn in an archival radio programme *Music Ho, Douglas Lilburn 50th Birthday Tribute* (Ngā Taonga Sound & Vision 1478).

3   The march is aptly described as 'patriarchal' in Wilfred Mellers, *Vaughan Williams and the Vision of Albion* (London: Barrie & Jenkins, 1989), p. 109; Lilburn became familiar with *Flos Campi* (1925) when studying with Ralph Vaughan Williams in London.

4   Gwyneth Brown in Concert FM programme *Douglas Lilburn: The Landscape of a New Zealand Composer*, produced by Roger Smith and Gareth Watkins, 2002.

5   Harris and Norman (eds), *Douglas Lilburn: A Festschrift*, p. 31.

6   Allen Curnow, 'Hamlet in Modern Dress', *New Zealand Listener*, 20 August 1943, p. 6.

7   Only the music for *Hamlet* and *Othello* survives.

8   Chris Bourke, 'Douglas Lilburn: An Interview', *Music in New Zealand* 31 (1995–96), p. 33.

9   Harris and Norman (eds), *Douglas Lilburn: A Festschrift*, p. 31.

10 Douglas Lilburn to Richard Campion. Archival interview recorded in 1989 (Ngā Taonga Sound & Vision 14358).

11 Douglas Lilburn to William Norrie Rogers, no date, Alexander Turnbull Library, MS-Papers-7623-277, quoted in Philip Norman, *Douglas Lilburn: His Life and Music* (Christchurch: Canterbury University Press, 2006), p. 118.

12 Pers. comm., David Sell to Robert Hoskins, winter 2013. Sell, on the music staff at the University of Canterbury, chaired the original Christchurch committee. For Lilburn's address, see Robert Hoskins (ed.), *Douglas Lilburn: Memories of Early Years and Other Writings* (Christchurch: Steele Roberts, 2014), pp. 60–71.

Incidental music for Hamlet
Douglas Lilburn

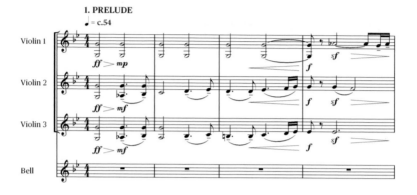

2. [FLOURISH]

3a. [MARCH]

4. PLAYERS' MUSIC

Enter PLAYER KING and PLAYER QUEEN

Repeat last section only if necessary

HORATIO:
Let four captains bear Hamlet, like a soldier, to the stage; for he was likely, had he been put on, to have proved most royally and, for his passage, the soldiers' music, and the rites of war, speak loudly for him.

5. FINALE

Largo